sewNEWS

the trusted sewing source

Q UICKLY REFRESH your couch cushions, bedroom set or reading nook with a simple swap of the pillows. Stitching new pillows or pillowcases is the easiest way to change up your home décor without spending a lot of time (or money). Plus, the embellishment and fabric choices are endless!

Turn the pages to find pillows galore that are simple enough to complete in no time yet exciting enough to impress your friends and family. Once you've updated every room in your home with fabulous new pillows, make some as gifts for any occasion.

Enjoy and have fun!

For more information, visit **sewnews.com.**

the art of everyday living
www.leisurearts.com

sewNEWS

741 Corporate Circle, Ste. A
Golden, CO, 80401
sewnews.com

SEW NEWS STAFF
Editorial
Editor-in-Chief: Ellen March
Senior Editor: Beth Bradley
Associate Editor: Nicole LaFoille
Web Editor: Jill Case
Editorial Assistant: Jessica Giardino

Art
Creative Director: Sue Dothage
Graphic Designer: Erin Hershey
Assistant Graphic Designer: Courtney Kraig
Illustrator: Melinda Bylow
Photography: Brent Ward, Jessica Grenier,
Mellisa Karlin Mahoney
Hair & Makeup Stylist: Angela Lewis

CREATIVE CRAFTS GROUP
**Group Publisher &
Community Leader:** Kristi Loeffelholz
VP of Content: Helen Gregory
Publisher: June Dudley

OPERATIONS
New Business Manager: Adriana Maldonado
Newsstand Consultant: TJ Montilli
Online Marketing Manager: Jodi Lee
Retail Sales: LaRita Godfrey: (800) 815-3538

F+W MEDIA INC.
Chairman & CEO: David Nussbaum
CFO & COO: James Ogle
President: Sara Domville
President: David Blansfield
Chief Digital Officer: Chad Phelps
VP/E-Commerce: Lucas Hilbert
Senior VP/Operations: Phil Graham
VP/Communications: Stacie Berger

LEISURE ARTS STAFF
Editorial Staff
Vice President of Editorial: Susan White Sullivan
Creative Art Director: Katherine Laughlin
Publications Director: Leah Lampirez
Special Projects Director: Susan Frantz Wiles
Prepress Technician: Stephanie Johnson

Business Staff
President and Chief Executive Officer:
Rick Barton
Senior Vice President of Operations:
Jim Dittrich
Vice President of Finance: Fred F. Pruss
Vice President of Sales-Retail Books:
Martha Adams
Vice President of Mass Market:
Bob Bewighouse
Vice President of Technology and Planning:
Laticia Mull Dittrich
Controller: Tiffany P. Childers
Information Technology Director: Brian Roden
Director of E-Commerce: Mark Hawkins
Manager of E-Commerce: Robert Young
Retail Customer Service Manager: Stan Raynor

Library of Congress Control Number: 2014937332
ISBN-13/EAN: 978-1-4647-1546-4
UPC: 0-28906-06314-1

contents

42

4

8

28

50

18

38

53

36

48

PILLOWS IN
BLOOM

{ by Kim Saba }

Add retro charm to any room with
chenille-trimmed pillows.

Diamond Pillow

Create a chenille grid emulating
diamond shapes across the pillow front.

Supplies
*Supplies listed are enough to make
one 16" square pillow.*

- 1 yard of mediumweight
  home-décor fabric

- 10 yards of ⅝"-wide
  chenille trim (See "Sources.")

- 18" square of mediumweight
  cut-away fusible stabilizer

- 16" square pillow form

- Tracing paper & wheel

- Matching all-purpose thread

- Hand sewing needle

- Chenille brush
  (optional; see "Sources")

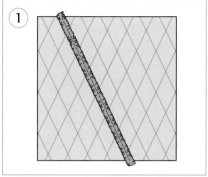

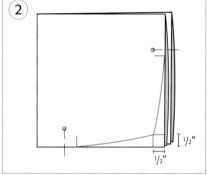

Cut

Prewash the fabric according to the manufacturer's suggestions.

Create a diamond pillow template using the photo above as a reference. Cut two 18" squares from the home-dec fabric. Designate one as the pillow front and one as the pillow back.

Center the stabilizer square over the pillow-front wrong side; fuse, following the manufacturer's instructions.

Position the pillow front right side up on a flat work surface. Position the tracing paper wrong side up over the pillow front. Position the template over the tracing paper, aligning the perimeter with the pillow front. Trace the diamond pattern using a tracing wheel.

Construct

Use ¹/₂″ seam allowances.

Cut the chenille trim length in half widthwise. With right sides up, stack one length over the other, aligning the short ends.

Center the trim over one center traced line, extending the ends just slightly beyond the pillow-front edge. For additional stability, pin the trim to the pillow front before stitching.

Topstitch along the trim center, ending the stitching at the opposite line end (1).

Trim the chenille at the pillow-front edge. Repeat to stitch the remaining lines in the same direction.

Repeat to stitch the remaining lines in the opposite direction.

Trim the excess stabilizer and chenille ends from the pillow-front perimeter.

Fold the pillow back in half lengthwise and widthwise with right sides together; pin.

Measure and mark the center of each unfolded edge. Measure and mark ¹/₂″ from the unfolded corner. Draw a slightly curved line from one center mark to the corner mark. Repeat for the opposite edge (2).

Cut along the lines. Unfold the pillow back. (Tapering the corners prevents a dog-eared pillow.)

With right sides together, align the pillow front and back; pin. Stitch the perimeter, leaving a centered 8″-long opening along one edge for turning.

Trim the pillow front corners to match the pillow back and clip the corners at a diagonal.

Turn the pillow right side out through the opening. Insert a ham or clapper into the pillowcase to press open the seam allowance for a crisp edge.

To fray the chenille, spray with water and rub a coarse brush or chenille brush over the trim. Or machine-wash the pillowcase in cold water and tumble dry on low heat. Multiple washes may be necessary to achieve the desired amount of fray.

Insert the pillow form through the opening. Slipstitch the opening closed.

Love Pillow

Spell out the word "love" on the pillow front for a sweet accent.

Supplies

Supplies listed are enough to make one 10"x16" pillow.

- 1/3 yard of mediumweight home-décor fabric
- 6 yards of 5/8"-wide chenille trim (See "Sources.")
- 12"x18" rectangle of mediumweight cut-away fusible stabilizer
- 10"x16" pillow form
- Tracing paper & wheel
- Matching all-purpose thread
- Hand sewing needle
- Chenille brush (optional; see "Sources")

Cut

Prewash the fabric according to the manufacturer's suggestions.

Create a love template using the photo at right for reference. Cut two 12" x 18" rectangles from the home-dec fabric. Designate one as the pillow front and one as the pillow back.

Center the stabilizer rectangle over the pillow-front wrong side; fuse following the manufacturer's instructions.

Position the pillow front right side up on a flat work surface. Position the tracing paper wrong side up over the pillow front. Position the template over the tracing paper, aligning the perimeter with the pillow front. Trace the pattern using a tracing wheel.

Construct

Use 1/2" seam allowances.

Cut the chenille trim length in half widthwise. With right sides up, stack one length over the other, aligning the short ends.

Position the short ends at the beginning of the letter "L," centering the trim over the line. Topstitch along the trim center, following the traced line. End stitching with the needle in the down position and lift the presser foot to adjust the trim to follow the tight curves in one continuous smooth line, overlapping the trim as necessary. End the stitching at the end of the letter "E"; trim the chenille close to the stitching.

Measure and mark 1⅛" from the pillow-front perimeter for the borderline.

Position the trim short ends at the pillow-front lower edge center along the borderline, centering the trim over the line. Begin topstitching along the trim center. End with the needle in the down position at the corner. Lift the presser foot and rotate the pillow front 90°, and then continue stitching the perimeter. Repeat to turn each corner. Lap the trim end ¼" over the beginning. Trim the chenille close to the stitching.

Trim the excess stabilizer from the pillow-front perimeter.

Fold, mark and trim the pillow-back corners per the "Diamond Pillow" instructions.

With right sides together, align the pillow front and back; pin. Stitch the perimeter, leaving a centered 8"-long opening along one edge for turning.

Trim the pillow-front corners to match the pillow back and clip the corners at a diagonal.

Turn the pillow right side out through the opening. Insert a ham or clapper into the pillowcase to press open the seam allowance for a crisp edge.

Fray the chenille following the "Diamond Pillow" instructions on page 4.

Insert the pillow form through the opening. Fold the opening seam allowances ½" toward the wrong side. Slipstitch the opening closed.

Swirl Pillow

Create a circular, tufted pillow with chenille swirls.

Supplies

Supplies listed are enough to make one 16"-diameter circle pillow.

- 1 yard of mediumweight home-décor fabric
- 16 yards of 5/8"-wide chenille trim (See "Sources.")
- 18" square of mediumweight cut-away fusible stabilizer
- 16"-diameter circle pillow form
- Tracing paper & wheel
- Thread: heavyweight & matching all-purpose
- Long hand sewing needle
- One 3/4"- & 1 1/2"-diameter covered button kit
- Chenille brush (optional; see "Sources")

Cut

Prewash the fabric according to the manufacturer's suggestions.

Create a swirl template using the photo at left for reference. Cut two 18" diameter circles from the home-dec fabric. Designate one as the pillow front and one as the pillow back.

Center the stabilizer rectangle over the pillow-front wrong side; fuse following the manufacturer's instructions.

Position the pillow front right side up on a flat work surface. Position the tracing paper wrong side up over the pillow front. Position the template over the tracing paper, aligning the perimeter with the pillow front. Trace the pattern using a tracing wheel.

Construct

Use 1/2" seam allowances.

Cut the chenille trim length in half widthwise. With right sides up, stack one length over the other, aligning the short ends.

Center the trim short ends over the line at the starting point on the pillow front right side. Topstitch along trim center, following the traced line. End with the needle in the down position and lift the presser foot to adjust the trim to follow the curves in one continuous line. End the stitching at the ending point along the pillow perimeter.

Trim the excess stabilizer from the pillow-front perimeter.

With right sides together, align the pillow front and back. Stitch the perimeter, leaving an 8"-long opening for turning. Clip into the seam allowance at 1" intervals.

Turn the pillow right side out through the opening. Insert a ham or clapper into the pillowcase to press open the seam allowance for a crisp edge.

Fray the chenille following the "Diamond Pillow" instructions on page 4.

Insert the pillow form through the opening. Fold the opening seam allowances 1/2" toward the wrong side. Slipstitch the opening closed.

Cover each button with home-dec fabric, following the covered button kit instructions.

Thread a hand sewing needle with a double length of heavyweight thread; knot the end.

Knot the thread around the large covered-button shank. Insert the needle into the pillow-front center and pull the needle through to the pillow-back center.

Thread the needle through the small covered-button shank. Insert the needle next to the previous hole and pull the needle through to the pillow-front center next to the first hole. Pull the thread taut for the desired pillow tuft. Wind the thread around the covered button shank; knot the end. Trim the thread close to the knot. ✂

SOURCES

Delta Patchwork provided the Chenille-It Blooming Bias: (877) 760-5916, deltapatchwork.com.

Nancy's Notions provided the Chenille Brush: (800) 833-0690, nancysnotions.com.

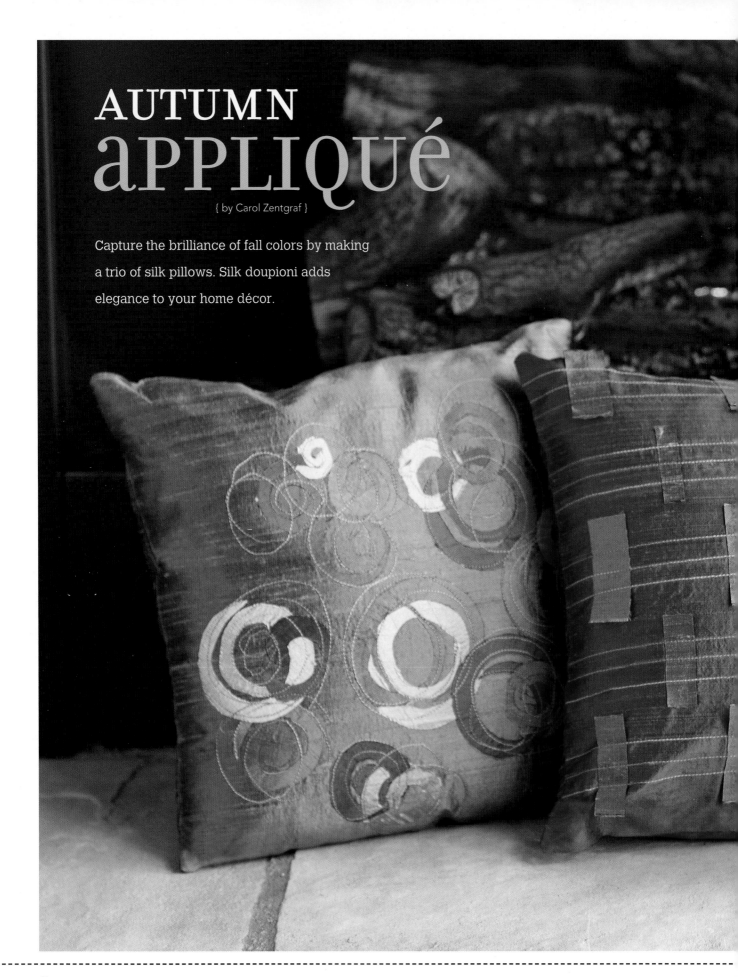

AUTUMN
APPLIQUÉ

{ by Carol Zentgraf }

Capture the brilliance of fall colors by making
a trio of silk pillows. Silk doupioni adds
elegance to your home décor.

Tip: Trace clipart leaves to create new templates for variety.

Leaves Pillow

Supplies

Supplies listed are enough to make one 14" square pillow.

- ⁷/₈ yard of silk doupioni
- 14" square pillow form
- ¹/₃ yard of fusible tricot interfacing
- Lightweight fusible web
- Thread: All-purpose & variegated 12-wt. cotton
- Chalk marker
- Press cloth
- Tracing paper

Cut

From the silk doupioni, cut two 15" squares, twelve 5" squares and one 8" x 12" rectangle.

From the fusible tricot interfacing, cut one 15" square.

From the lightweight fusible web, cut twelve 5" squares.

Embellish

Fuse the interfacing square to one large doupioni square wrong side, following the manufacturer's instructions. This will be the embellished panel.

Position the fusible web squares on the small doupioni square wrong sides; fuse, using a press cloth.

Trace the leaf template from page 64 onto tracing paper; cut out. Draw one leaf onto the interfaced side of each 5" square; cut out. Draw leaf veins on each leaf right side using a chalk marker.

Arrange the leaves on the interfaced doupioni square right side, as desired. Once satisfied with the placement, fuse only the stem and center of each leaf. Note: If you accidentally fuse the leaf, gently peel away the leaf edges while warm.

Thread the machine needle with variegated cotton thread. Stitch along the stem and leaf vein marks using a straight stitch.

Construct

With wrong sides together, align the embellished square with the remaining doupioni square; pin, and then stitch using a ¹/₂" seam allowance. Leave an 8" opening along one edge for turning.

Finish

Turn the pillow cover right side out through the opening. Fold the opening edges ¹/₂" toward the wrong side; press. Insert the pillow form through the opening; slipstitch the opening closed.

Swirls Pillow

Supplies

Supplies listed are enough to make one 14" square pillow.

- ⁷/₈ yard of silk doupioni
- 14" square pillow form
- ¹/₃ yard of fusible tricot interfacing
- Lightweight fusible web
- Thread: All-purpose & variegated 12-wt. cotton
- Press cloth
- Tracing paper

Cut

From the silk doupioni, cut two 15" squares and seventeen 2" to 4" squares, varying the sizes as desired.

From the fusible tricot interfacing, cut one 15" square.

From the lightweight fusible web, cut squares that correspond with the small doupioni squares.

Embellish

Fuse the interfacing square to one large doupioni square wrong side. This will be the embellished panel.

Position the fusible web squares on the small doupioni square wrong sides; fuse, using a press cloth.

Using a removable fabric marker, free-hand draw a circle onto the interfaced side of each small doupioni square, varying the sizes and shapes. Cut out each circle in a spiral, cutting away the center from several circles (see photo on page 11).

Arrange the circles on the interfaced doupioni square right side, overlapping as desired. Once satisfied with the placement, fuse the circles in place.

Set the machine for free-motion stitching; thread with variegated cotton thread. Stitch the circles, stitching partially onto the background fabric, as desired (see photo on page 11).

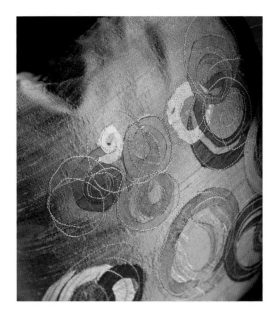

Tip: Instead of tabs, cut triangles, hearts, stars or other shapes.

Finish constructing the pillow as for "Leaves Pillow" on page 10.

Tabs Pillow

Supplies

Supplies listed are enough to make one 14" square pillow.

- ½ yard of silk doupioni
- ¼ yard each of 3 coordinating silk doupioni fabrics
- 14" square pillow form
- ⅓ yard of fusible tricot interfacing
- Lightweight fusible web
- 8" x 12" sheet of double-sided paper-backed fusible web
- Thread: All-purpose & variegated 12-wt. cotton
- Permanent fabric glue (See "Sources.")
- Chalk marker
- Tracing paper

Cut

From the ½ yard of silk doupioni, cut two 15" squares.

From each of the coordinating doupioni fabrics, cut two 6" x 8" rectangles.

From the fusible tricot interfacing, cut one 15" square.

From the fusible web, cut three 6" x 8" rectangles.

Embellish

Fuse the tricot square to one doupioni square wrong side. This will be the embellished panel.

Position the fusible web on the doupioni rectangle wrong sides; fuse, using a press cloth. Remove the paper backing, and then position the remaining doupioni rectangle over the fusible web with the right side facing up; fuse. Trim, if necessary. Repeat to fuse the remaining rectangles.

From each double-sided silk rectangle, cut ½"- to 1¼"-wide x 2½"- to 3"-long rectangles for the tabs (vary the lengths and widths).

Position the interfaced pillow square right side up on a flat work surface. Designate one edge as the upper edge. Using a chalk marker, draw a horizontal straight line 1½" from the upper edge.

Draw another line ½" below the first line, and then draw another line ½" below the previous line. Draw another set of three lines 1½" below the first set. Repeat to draw lines across the entire square.

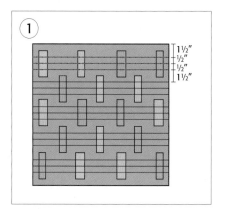

Arrange the tabs over the drawn lines, as desired. Once satisfied with the placement, secure each tab using permanent spray adhesive; let dry.

Thread the machine needle with variegated cotton thread. Straight stitch along the lines over the tabs (1). Finish constructing the pillow as for "Leaves Pillow" on page 10. ❧

SOURCES

Beacon Adhesives provided Fabri-Tac permanent fabric adhesive: (914) 699-3405, beaconcreates.com.

Fairfield Processing Corporation provided Soft Touch pillow forms: (800) 980-8000, poly-fil.com.

Mistyfuse provided sheer Mistyfuse permanent fabric glue and Goddess Press Sheets: (631) 750-8500, mistyfuse.com.

Sulky of America provided 12-wt. variegated cotton thread: (800) 874-4115, sulky.com.

Thai Silks provided silk doupioni fabric: (800) 722-7455, thaisilks.com.

The Warm Company provided Steam A Seam 2 paper-backed fusible web: (425) 248-2424, warmcompany.com.

Eastern
INFLUENCE

{ by Shannon Okey }

Beautiful silk fabric brings to mind
traditional Eastern dress. Make a simple
kimono-inspired silk obi to wrap a pillow
for lots of chic decorating options.

Kanji character
for Lucky Person

果
報
者

Tip: Save time by using ready-made coordinating silk ribbon or cording to secure the obi around the pillow.

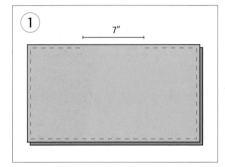

① 7"

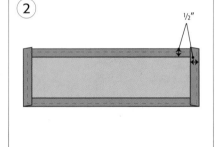

② ½"

Supplies

Use ½" seam allowances unless otherwise noted.

- 12"x15" rectangular pillow form
- ½ yard of silk fabric (fabric A)
- 11"x28" rectangle of coordinating silk fabric (fabric B)
- Matching all-purpose thread
- Two decorative ½"-diameter buttons

Cut & Construct

From fabric A, cut two 12"x16" rectangles and one 1½"x22" strip.

To create the pillowcase, position the two fabric A rectangles with right sides facing. Beginning on one long edge, stitch around the rectangle perimeter, leaving a 7" opening for turning (1). Clip the corners.

Turn the pillowcase right side out; press the edges. Insert the pillow form.

Slipstitch the opening closed.

To create the obi, fold the fabric B rectangle long edges 1½" toward the wrong side; press. Fold the short edges 1½" toward the wrong side; press.

Topstitch around the obi perimeter (2).

Center one button along one obi short edge on the fabric right side. Hand stitch the button in place. Repeat for the other obi short edge.

To create the tie, fold the fabric A strip in half lengthwise with right sides facing; press. Stitch the long open edge using a ¼" seam allowance.

Trim the seam allowance. Use a tube turner to turn the strip right side out; press. Finish both tie ends with a knot.

Wrap the obi around the pillow, aligning the buttons and short edges. Wind the tie around the buttons to secure the obi; tie a bow or knot as desired. ✄

QUICK SWITCH

For more décor choices, make the obi reversible.

- Cut one obi rectangle each from two different fabrics.
- Pin the rectangles together with right sides facing. Stitch around the rectangle perimeter, leaving a 5" opening for turning along one long edge.
- Turn the obi right side out. Press the edges, turning in the opening edges. Topstitch around the obi perimeter, making sure to catch the opening seam allowance.
- Stitch buttons on both sides of the obi for fastening.

PILLOW
TALK
{ by Pam Archer }

Add a wrap to an old pillow for an instant home makeover.

Pillows are great accessories. They readily tie different colors and textures together and add decorative dimension to a room. But did you know that pillows can have a wardrobe all their own? Take a look at these quick-to-sew pillow wraps that turn everyday pillows into make-a-statement accessories.

Supplies

- 18"-square pillow

- 1/3 to 3/4 yard of 45"-wide fashion fabric (as listed per project)

- 5 1/4" of 5/8"-wide hook-and-loop tape

- Fabric glue

- Matching all-purpose thread

- Fabric marking pencil or air-soluble marker

Finished size is 5 1/2"x36 1/2". Read the full instructions for each wrap prior to construction.

Basic Construction

Cut a 12"x 37 1/2" rectangle from the specified fabric. Fold under the short ends 1/2"; press.

With right sides together, fold the rectangle in half, aligning the long edges; pin. Using a 1/2" seam allowance, stitch along the pinned edge. Press the seam open.

Turn the wrap right side out, centering the seam on the back. Press the wrap flat; edgestitch.

On the wrap front side, apply a bead of glue along the edge of one short end. Finger-press one portion of the hook-and-loop tape into the glue.

Turn the wrap over, and apply a bead of glue at the opposite short end.

Finger-press the corresponding strip of hook-and-loop tape into the glue and let dry. If you prefer, stitch the hook-and-loop tape instead of gluing.

Asian Wrap

Supplies

- 1/3 yard of 45"-wide Asian-themed fabric

- 1 yard of fusible interfacing

- 3 1/2"-long beaded tassel

- Two 2 1/2" lengths of 1/2"-wide fusible adhesive strip

- One 5/8"-diameter, self-adhesive hook-and-loop tape dot

Cut one 5 1/2"x36" rectangle from the fusible interfacing.

Center and fuse the interfacing to the wrap wrong side.

Construct the basic pillow wrap, stopping before the hook-and-loop tape application.

Create end points by folding the corners on each short end to the back center seam (1).

Place one fusible strip along the point's hemline (2). Fuse in place following the manufacturer's instructions. Repeat for the other end.

Place the wrap around the pillow bringing the points to the front. Overlap the points 1", and mark with an air-soluble marking pen.

Apply the hook-and-loop tape dots at the overlap markings. Stitch the beaded tassel to the overlapping point.

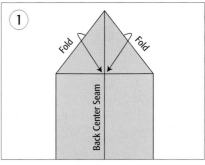

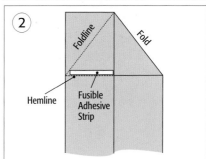

Plaid Tab Wrap

Supplies

- ⅓ yard of plaid fabric
- Three 1½″ coverable buttons
- One 6″x16″ faux-suede strip

Cut two faux-suede triangles measuring 5½″ at the base and 4½″ tall.

Cut three faux-suede circles, and use them to cover the buttons following the manufacturer's instructions.

Modify the basic wrap by tapering in the seam at each end. Beginning 2½″ from each short end, gradually increase the seam allowance to ¾″. Apply the hook–and–loop tape after the faux suede triangle is applied.

Turn the wrap wrong side up. Apply a bead of fabric-basting glue along the hem.

Place the base of one triangle right side up on the glue, overlapping the edges ¼″. Gently finger-press the base in place and allow to dry.

Turn the wrap over, and glue the second triangle, aligning the raw edges with the first triangle. Allow the glue to dry before stitching.

Edgestitch the triangles together through all layers (3). Trim any uneven edges.

Stitch on the buttons, spacing them 1″ apart, and beginning 1¼″ from the triangle's base (4).

With the right side facing up, apply the hook strip of the hook-and-loop tape to one short end. Apply the loop portion to the wrap wrong side just above the flap, abutting the edges.

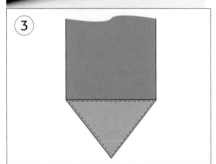

③

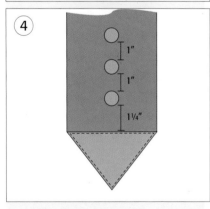

④

1″

1″

1¼″

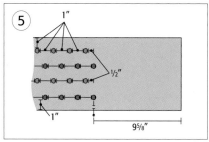

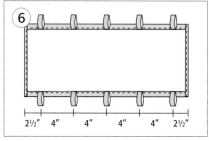

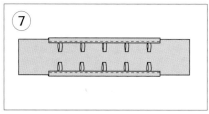

Beaded Wrap

Supplies

- $\frac{1}{3}$ yard of 45"- or 54"-wide striped chenille
- 66 assorted colored beads, size 8
- Hand-sewing needle

Make the basic wrap as directed. To determine the wrap's beading area, place a pin $9\frac{5}{8}$" from each short end.

With a double-threaded needle, begin beading at the pin. Stitch the beads with a running stitch, taking a stitch through the upper fabric layer, through the bead and directly back through the top fabric layer, in 1" intervals.

Stagger the beads for the second row by placing the first bead $\frac{1}{2}$" in from the pin. Stitch using the same 1" intervals between each bead. Continue a staggered pattern for the third and fourth rows (5).

Woven Ribbon Wrap

Supplies

- $\frac{3}{4}$ yard of 45"-wide mini-check fabric
- $2\frac{1}{4}$ yards of $\frac{3}{8}$"-wide coordinating ribbon

Construct the basic pillow wrap.

Cut a $9\frac{1}{4}$"x21$\frac{3}{4}$" rectangle from the fabric. Also cut a 2"x28" bias fabric strip to make the loops.

To make the looped band, serge or zigzag the edges of the $9\frac{1}{4}$"x21$\frac{3}{4}$" rectangle. Fold under the long edges $\frac{3}{4}$", and topstitch $\frac{1}{2}$" from the fold. Turn under each short end $\frac{1}{2}$" and topstitch in place. Set the band aside.

To make the loops, fold the bias strip in half lengthwise with right sides together; pin. Stitch with a $\frac{1}{2}$" seam allowance. Trim the seam to $\frac{1}{4}$" and turn the tube right side out; press.

Cut the tube into ten $2\frac{1}{2}$"-long strips. Place the hemmed rectangle wrong side up. Along each long edge, mark a dot $2\frac{1}{2}$" from one short end, a second dot

4" from the first, and three more dots each 4" apart.

Fold each bias strip in half to form a loop, and place a loop at each mark, matching the raw edges (6). Secure the loops by stitching across the ends, following the previous stitching lines.

Wrong sides together, center the pillow wrap over the band. Fold each looped band edge $1\frac{1}{8}$" to the wrap right side.

Sew along the previous stitching lines through all layers (7). Repeat on the remaining side.

Thread the ribbon through the loops like a shoelace, crisscrossing the ribbon between the loops. Tie the remaining length into a bow.

Encircle the pillow with the completed wrap, securing at the back with the hook-and-loop tape. ✄

SOURCES
Crafters Pick "The Ultimate" Adhesive Products, Inc. provided the fabric glue. craferspick.com.
Husqvarna Viking provided the sewing machine used to construct the pillow wraps. husqvarnaviking.com.
The Warm Company provided the Steam-A-Seam 2 Iron-on Adhesive. warmcompany.com.

PILLOWS
A-PLENTY

{ by Cheryl Stranges }

Dress up your décor with a collection of
pretty textured pillows featuring easily
gathered panels.

Gorgeous Gathers

A serger equipped with a differential feed option saves time on projects that require a gathered edge. The differential feed controls the dual feed dogs at different rates, bunching woven fabric beneath the needle. While conventional gathering techniques require several steps, including basting and manually distributing the fabric, a serger gathers and finishes the fabric edge in one easy step. Sergers vary in terms of needle tension and differential feed settings for gathering, so refer to the machine manual for the manufacturer's recommendations. Specialty serger presser feet and attachments are also available through machine dealers. Before beginning a project, practice gathering fabric scraps to determine the tension and feed settings that are most effective for various fabric weights and types.

Note: Use a $\frac{1}{4}''$ seam allowance for each pillow.

Hip Strips

Gather four fabric strips to create a simple square pillow.

Supplies

- **1 yard of mediumweight cream fabric**
- **$4\frac{1}{2}''$x the fabric width strip each of mediumweight green and pink fabric**
- **Coordinating serger thread**
- **Polyester fiberfill**
- **Temporary spray adhesive**
- **Hand sewing needle**

Cut

From the cream fabric, cut two 16″ squares and two $4\frac{1}{2}''$x the fabric width strips.

Serge

Set the serger feed and needle tension for a 4-thread gathering stitch on a double fabric layer, following the manufacturer's instructions.

With right sides together, pin the green strip and one cream strip along one long edge; serge, leaving long thread tails.

With right sides together, pin the remaining cream strip over the green strip, aligning the long raw edges; serge. Repeat to attach the pink strip to the second cream strip long raw edge.

Set the serger to gather a single fabric layer. Serge the remaining pink and first cream strip long raw edges. Adjust the stitches to evenly distribute the gathers, forming 16″-long strips **(1)**.

Spray one cream square right side with temporary spray adhesive. Position the gathered panel right side up over the cream square; finger-press to adhere.

With right sides together, serge the remaining cream square and gathered panel perimeter, leaving a 4″ opening along one edge for turning. Clip the corners.

Finish

Turn the pillow right side out and stuff it with fiberfill until plump. Hand stitch the opening closed.

Tip: Create a commemorative wedding pillow by stitching the bride and groom's names on each panel.

Puckered Panache

Choose initials, a favorite phrase, or two coordinating embroidery designs to spice up this pillow design.

Supplies

- ½ yard of mediumweight green fabric
- 4"x the fabric width strip of cream fabric
- Temporary spray adhesive
- Polyester fiberfill
- Hand sewing needle
- Thread: coordinating serger and embroidery (optional)
- Embroidery lettering design (optional)
- Fusible tear-away stabilizer (optional)

Prepare

From the green fabric, cut two 6½"x9" rectangles and one 9"x16" rectangle.

Cut the cream strip into one 4"x9" strip and one 4"x32" strip.

Select a design or phrase on the embroidery machine to stitch a phrase at each small rectangle center. Adhere tear-away stabilizer to each rectangle wrong side, using temporary spray adhesive. Hoop each rectangle, and then stitch the selected design using coordinating embroidery thread. Un-hoop the rectangles and tear away the stabilizer; press.

Construct

Set the serger to gather a single fabric layer. Serge the cream strip long edges, leaving long thread tails. Adjust the gathers until the strip is 9" long.

Spray the short cream strip right side with temporary spray adhesive. Place the gathered strip right side up over the short strip, aligning the outer edges; finger-press to adhere (2). Stitch the perimeter.

With right sides together, position one small green rectangle over the gathered strip, aligning one long edge; serge. Repeat to attach the remaining

small green rectangle to the opposite gathered strip edge (3). Press the seams toward the green rectangles.

With right sides together, serge the pillow front and large rectangle perimeter, leaving a 4" opening on one long edge for turning. Clip the corners.

Finish

Turn the pillow right side out. Stuff it with fiberfill until plump. Hand stitch the opening closed.

Romantic Ruffles

Ruffles and lace make a flouncy feminine statement.

Supplies

- ½ yard of mediumweight cream fabric
- Three 4"x the fabric width strips of mediumweight pink fabric
- 1 yard of 2"-wide lace
- Thread: Coordinating serger and multi-colored decorative
- Polyester fiberfill
- Hand sewing needle
- Removable fabric marker
- Fabric adhesive

Cut

From the cream fabric, cut one 10½"x17" rectangle and four 5"x10½" rectangles.

Fold one small rectangle in half widthwise; mark the center along one long edge. Mark the short edges 2″ from the marks. Connect each 2″ mark to the long-edge center mark. Cut along the lines to create the upper triangle.

Position the upper triangle over the large rectangle, aligning the triangle point with one short edge. Trace the triangle upper edge onto the large rectangle. Cut along the lines. This is the pillow back.

Cut the lace into three 10½″-long pieces.

Construct

Set the serger for a 2-thread chainstitch. Thread the needle with serger thread and the looper with decorative thread. With the wrong side facing up, stitch a wavy line lengthwise along each pink strip.

Set the serger for a 3-thread rolled edge and thread the serger with coordinating thread. Serge one long edge of each pink strip.

Set the serger to gather a single fabric layer. Serge each pink strip long raw edge, leaving long thread tails. Adjust the gathers until each ruffle is 10½″ long (4).

Position one small rectangle right side up. Position one ruffle right side up over the rectangle, aligning the gathered edge with one rectangle long edge. Layer a second small rectangle right side down over the ruffle; serge the long edge. Unfold and repeat to attach the remaining ruffles, rectangle and upper triangle (5).

Position one lace piece 2″ from the triangle point so the lace lower edge overlaps the ruffle by ½″. Stitch or glue the lace in place.

Position the second lace piece 3″ from the center rectangle upper edge; stitch or glue in place. Repeat to attach the remaining lace piece to the second center rectangle.

Finish

With right sides together, serge the pillow front and back perimeter, making sure the ruffles remain tucked between the fabric layers. Leave a 3″ opening along the short straight edge for turning.

Clip the corners. Turn the pillow right side out. Stuff it with fiberfill until plump. Hand stitch the opening closed. ✺

SOURCE
Husqvarna Viking provided the 936 Serger and Designer Diamond and Sapphire 870 sewing machines: (800) 358-0001, husqvarnaviking.com.
JN Harper Co Ltd. provided the Robert Kaufman Marbelous fabrics: jnharper.com.
Sulky provided thread and stabilizer: (800) 874-4115, sulky.com.

CHARMING CHAINSTITCH

Use the serger chainstitch function to create unique buttons and embellishments to decorate coordinating envelope pillows.

Supplies

- ½ yard of mediumweight fabric
- Thread: coordinating all-purpose, 60-wt. variegated embroidery
- Fusible tear-away stabilizer
- Polyester fiberfill
- Removable fabric marker
- Pom-pom tool (such as the Loop-de-Doodle)
- Hand sewing needle
- Fabric adhesive

Copy and enlarge the Elegant Envelope pattern from page 23. From the fabric, cut two pillows and two flaps. From the stabilizer, cut one flap.

Designate one fabric flap for chainstitching. Use the removable fabric marker to transfer the chainstitch grid from the pattern onto the flap wrong side. Fuse the stabilizer to the fabric flap wrong side.

Set the serger to a 2-thread chainstitch. Thread the needle with all-purpose thread and the looper with embroidery thread. With the wrong side facing up, stitch the flap over the gridlines **(A)**. The chainstitch will appear on the fabric right side.

Set the serger to a 4-thread overlock stitch. With right sides together, serge the flap side and lower edges. Clip the corners and turn the flap right side out.

Position one pillow right side up. Place the flap right side up over the pillow, aligning one long edge. Position the remaining pillow right side down, sandwiching the flap; pin.

Serge the pillow perimeter, leaving a 3" opening along the lower edge for turning. Clip the corners.

Turn the pillow right side out. Stuff with fiberfill until plump. Hand stitch the opening closed.

To make the button, begin chainstitching on a 1½"-square fabric scrap. Continue stitching until you have 10 yards of chainstitched thread **(B)**.

Wrap the pom-pom tool with the thread. Stitch down the thread center **(C)**.

Remove the looped thread from the tool. Twist the looped thread into a 2½"-diameter circle **(D)**.

Cut one 2½"-diameter circle each from the fabric and stabilizer. Fuse the stabilizer to the fabric wrong side. Glue the thread circle to the fabric circle wrong side. Hand stitch or glue the button to the pillow flap.

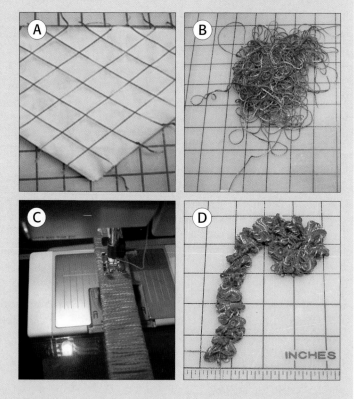

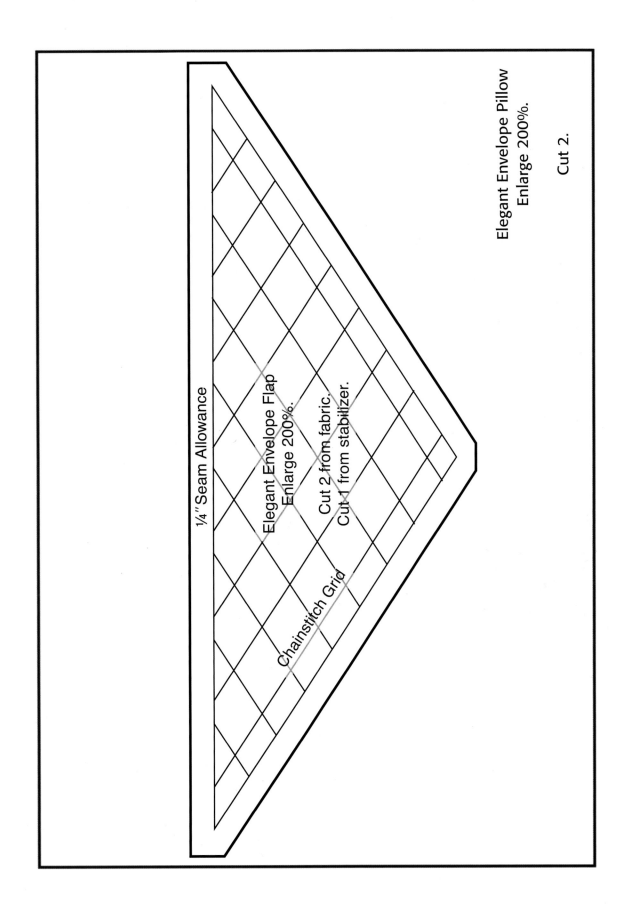

Elegant Envelope Pillow
Enlarge 200%.

Cut 2.

¼" Seam Allowance

Elegant Envelope Flap
Enlarge 200%.

Cut 2 from fabric.
Cut 1 from stabilizer.

Chainstitch Grid

RETHINKING WOOL

{ by Linda Lee }

Not just for coats and blankets, wool is the perfect fabric for easy-to-sew pillow construction.

When looking for pillow fabric, most people head to the decorator department of the fabric store, but scouring your stash of garment fabrics instead can be just the ticket. Remnants from coats, sweaters, blazers and other winter-wear offer up all kinds of new possibilities for pillow making.

Simple details, minimal embellishments, and best of all, the ability to use raw edges, highlight the natural beauty of wool and make it a genuine candidate for any season.

Fabrics

Look for wool fabric that doesn't ravel much, such as double-faced wool, which usually has a different color on each side. Another good choice is a heavyweight coating, such as melton or soft cashmere blends.

Or look for fabric that shrinks and no longer ravels when repeatedly washed and dried. This includes single-knit wool jerseys and sweater knits (including old sweaters that no longer fit or are out of style).

To felt wool fabrics, wash them in the hottest water without detergent, and agitate on the longest cycle. After the first laundering, dry in a hot dryer. Check the amount of felting and shrinking. If you want a denser look or more texture, continue washing and agitating until the fabric is felted how you want it. This can take as many as five or six washings.

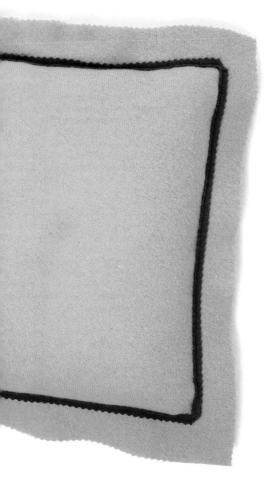

Warm & Wooly Pillows

Supplies

Supplies listed are enough to make one pillow.

- $\frac{2}{3}$ yard each of two colors of fabric (after felting)
- $\frac{1}{8}$ yard of felted wool jersey or 2 yards of $1\frac{1}{2}$″-wide ribbon
- Rotary cutter with pinking blade or pinking shears
- $\frac{1}{8}$″-wide double-sided tape or narrow strips of fusible web
- 16″-square pillow form
- Matching thread
- Chalk marker

Wool Jersey Trim

Cut one 23″ square from each color fabric. Using the rotary blade or pinking shears, cut enough $\frac{3}{8}$″-wide strips of felted wool jersey to equal two yards.

Chalk-mark a 16″ square in the center of one fabric square right side. Adhere strips of double-sided tape on the chalk marks. Center the wool jersey strips on the tape, overlapping the ends and turning the trim at right angles at each corner.

Wrong sides together, place the pillow squares together; pin three sides along the trim. Stitch down the center of the trim through all layers, leaving one side free to insert the pillow form **(1)**.

Insert the pillow form. Pin and sew the remaining side closed.

Using the rotary blade or pinking shears, cut the edges of both pillow layers the desired flange width.

Ribbon Trim

Cut one 23″ square from each color fabric.

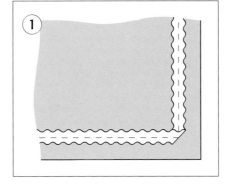

Chalk-mark a 16″ square in the center of one fabric square. Position fusible web strips outside the chalk lines.

Starting in one corner and extending about 3″ of ribbon beyond the corner, place the ribbon on the fusible web along one edge; fuse in place.

Miter the corner and continue fusing the ribbon to each side. Miter the final corner as detailed in "The Miter Touch" on page 27.

Edgestitch along the ribbon outer edge.

Wrong sides together, pin the two fabric squares together. Stitch along the ribbon inside edge on three sides.

Insert the pillow form. Pin the last side and sew along the ribbon inside edge to close.

Stitch along the ribbon outer edges, stitching only through the upper fabric layer.

Tip: Using down and feather pillow forms increases the luxury look of wool pillows. Cut the pillow fabrics the same size or slightly smaller than the form without adding seam allowances.

Western Girl Pillows

Supplies

Supplies listed are enough to make one pillow.

- 1 yard of double-faced wool
- 3 yards of white polyester cable cord
- Size 16 tapestry needle
- Chalk marker
- Clear ruler
- Rotary cutter
- Matching thread
- 18"-square down pillow form

Cut

From the double-faced wool, cut two 18" squares. Chalk-mark a line 1" from and parallel to each edge of one fabric square. Thread the tapestry needle with a length of cable cord. Knot one end, and sew long running stitches along the chalk marks **(2)**.

Cut four 3³/₄"x17" wool strips. Staystitch ¹/₂" from one long edge of each strip. Using a rotary cutter, cut ¹/₂"-wide fringe along each strip, starting at the raw edge and cutting to the staystitching line.

Construct

Use ¹/₂" seam allowances unless otherwise noted.

Right sides together, pin one fringe strip to one fabric square edge, centering the fringe and aligning the uncut edge with the square raw edge. Repeat, pinning the remaining fringe strips to the square edges **(3)**.

Pin the fringe ends out of the way at each corner. With right sides together, sew the two pillow squares together along three edges, sandwiching the fringe between the two layers.

Insert the pillow form. Turn the raw edges of the opening to the inside and slipstitch the opening closed. ✄

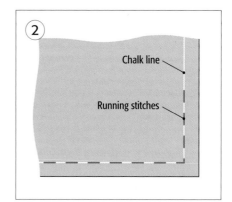

② Chalk line · Running stitches

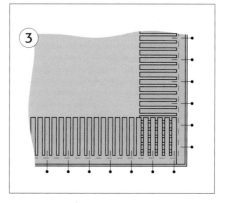

③

THE MITER TOUCH

- **Beginning a few inches** from one corner, stitch along the ribbon inner edge through the ribbon and the fabric square, stopping at the point where the ribbon will turn a right angle **(A)**.

- **Fold the trim back** on itself, aligning the fold 1½" from the last stitch. Draw a diagonal line from the last stitch on the inner edge to the corner point of the ribbon **(B)**.

- **Using the drawn line** as a guide, stitch a line with about a 1/16" bow to it through all layers **(C)**. Trim the folded ribbon to ¼".

- **Continue sewing** the ribbon inner edge to the next corner **(D)**. Repeat the previous steps to miter the

corner. Stop stitching a few inches before the final corner.

- **To complete the final corner,** place one piece of ribbon over the other at a right angle. Draw a line on the ribbon from the intersection of the inner corner to the outer corner **(E)**.

- **Reverse the ribbon** strips and mark a line from the inner corner to the outer corner **(F)**.

- **With right sides together,** match the drawn lines and stitch through the ribbon only **(G)**.

- **Trim the excess ribbon** and press to one side. Complete the stitching along the ribbon inner edge **(H)**.

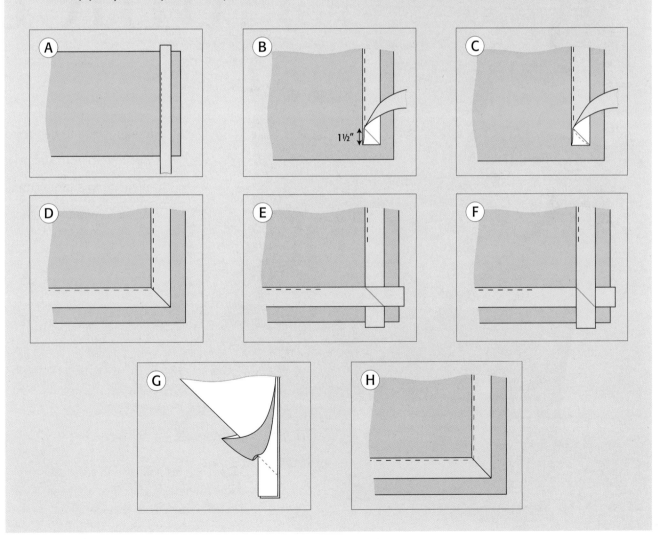

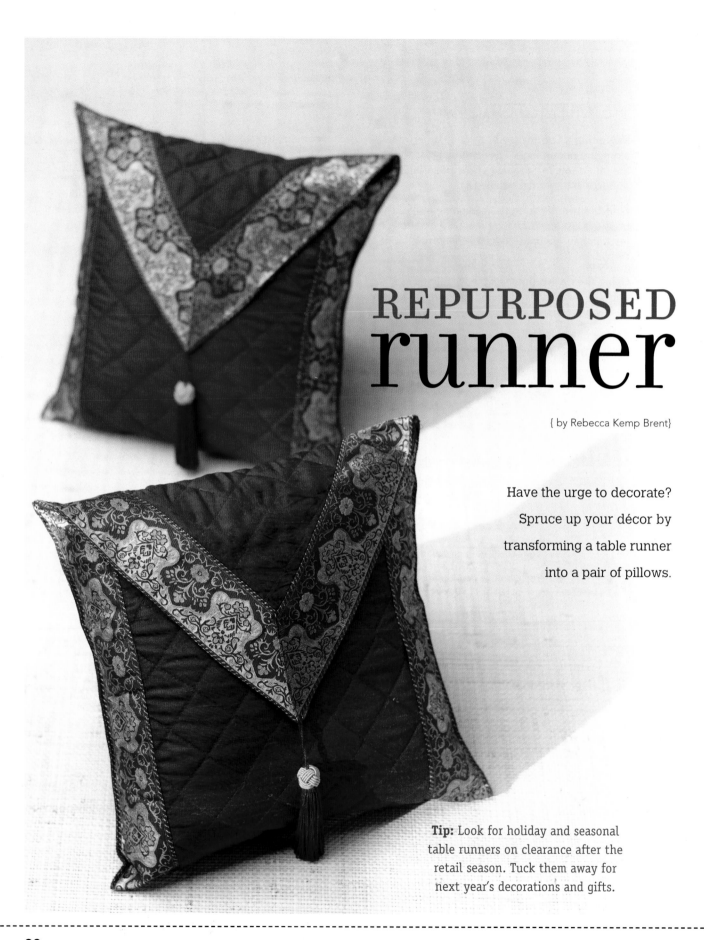

REPURPOSED
runner

{ by Rebecca Kemp Brent}

Have the urge to decorate?
Spruce up your décor by
transforming a table runner
into a pair of pillows.

Tip: Look for holiday and seasonal
table runners on clearance after the
retail season. Tuck them away for
next year's decorations and gifts.

Tip: If a table runner has corded edges, join the layers by stitching in the ditch along the cording.

Supplies

- Table runner with tasseled, tapered ends, about 14"x70"
- Matching all-purpose thread
- Two 14"-square pillow forms
- Water- or air-soluble marking pen

Construct

Cut the runner in half widthwise and serge or overcast the cut edges. Each half will make one pillow.

With wrong sides together fold in the finished edge approximately 14", aligning it with the base of the runner's tapered end (1). The exact measurement will vary.

Stitch the sides together using a zigzag stitch (3.5 mm wide, 1.4 mm long), overcast the edges, or straight stitch along the runner edges (2). Backstitch at the opening for reinforcement.

With a fabric-marking pen, draw a line on the runner wrong side along the finished cut end (3). This will act as a placement guide when stitching the pillow closed.

Insert a pillow form and compress it away from the opening. Pin the finished cut end to the runner along the marked line; stitch by hand or machine to secure.

Fluff the pillow form to fill the cushion.

Fold the tasseled end to the pillow front to create an envelope design.

Repeat to make a matching pillow from the remaining table runner half. ✂

OTHER IDEAS

- Embellish a plain table runner with machine embroidery or appliqué designs. Since many runners with tapered ends have a seam at the point center, choose a pair of motifs to place on either side and avoid stitching through the bulky seam allowances.

- If your runner lacks a tassel, make one from yarn, bullion fringe or beads.

- Add handles and omit the pillow form to create a tote from the table runner. Add body by backing the runner with stiff fusible interfacing before stitching.

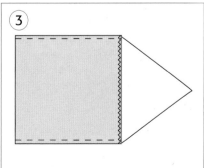

① Fold. Finished Cut Edge. Approx. 14"

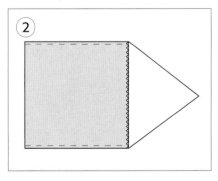

②

③

SASSY

{ by Shannon Mullen }

CHIC

Make this monogrammed pillowcase to brighten up any room.

Tip: To make the letter appliqué find a font you like from your computer and type the letter on a blank page on the screen.

Moving into a new apartment? Looking for a unique way to decorate your dorm room? Pillows are great accessories that add color and individuality to any space while keeping costs to a minimum. You can easily make sassy pillowcases to liven up your new place.

Supplies

- **1 yard of base fabric**
- **½ yard of contrasting fabric**
- **1½ yards of ³/₁₆″-wide home-dec cording**
- **Paper-backed fusible web**
- **Tear-away stabilizer**
- **Single-welt cording foot**
- **Clear presser foot**
- **Appliqué pressing sheet**
- **Coordinating all-purpose thread**

Cut

From the base fabric cut one 14″ square (for continuous bias tape), two 11″x15″ rectangles (back flaps) and one 11″ square (pillow front).

PIPING

Make continuous bias tape using the 14″ base fabric square. (For information on how to make continuous bias tape see "Floor Seating" on page 38.)

Lay the bias tape right side down and place the cording in the center. Fold the fabric around the cording.

Install the single-welt cording foot. Place the wrapped cording under the cording foot with the cording laying in the large tunnel on the left side. Select a straight stitch and move the needle three positions to the left or as close to the cording as possible. Stitch, allowing the machine to feed the cording through (if you don't have a cording foot use a zipper foot and stitch close to the enclosed cording). Set the finished piping aside.

LETTER APPLIQUÉ

Find a font you like from your computer and type the letter you wish to monogram on a blank page on the screen. Enlarge the letter to the desired size. Print the letter onto paper.

Cut a fusible-web square large enough to accommodate the letter. Trace the letter onto the paper side of the fusible web reversing the letter if it isn't symmetrical.

Following the manufacturer's instructions and using the appliqué pressing sheet, fuse the web to the appliqué fabric wrong side. Press lightly and move quickly to avoid burning the fabric; remove the pressing sheet.

Cut out the letter from the fabric and peel off the paper backing.

Center the letter on the 11″ square. Using the pressing sheet to protect the fabric and iron, press the letter onto the base fabric.

Cut two layers of tear-away stabilizer. Place the appliquéd square right side up on the tear-away stabilizer.

Install a clear presser foot to see the stitching path on the letter more clearly. Select a decorative stitch and sew around the letter.

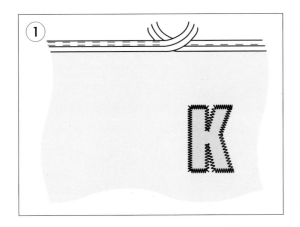

Tip: To make piping lay more smoothly around corners, stop and start stitching ½" from each corner and clip the seam allowance almost to the stitching.

Remove the stabilizer completely from the appliquéd square wrong side. Using a press cloth, press the 11" square. Use a firm up and down motion instead of a back and forth motion to avoid distorting the fabric.

Construct
BACK FLAP
Fold under one short edge of each rectangle ¼". Press the fold using a press cloth.

Remove the clear foot and install a straight-stitch foot.

Stitch close to the fold on both rectangles. Fold under the finished edge 2½"; press using a press cloth. Stitch over the previous stitching.

PILLOWCASE
Install the single-welt cording foot.

Pin the piping to the appliquéd square with raw edges aligned. Leave 2" free at each piping end.

Move the needle position to the left three times or as close to the piping as possible. Stitch close to the piping using a straight stitch.

Pull one piping end to the outside of the pillow, away from the letter. Stitch the opposite piping end down over the outside end. Then gradually pull that end away from the letter to the outside of the pillow while straight stitching **(1)**. This will create a beautiful and almost invisible finish.

Place the back flap pieces right sides together, making sure the 11" raw edges are facing opposite directions. Overlap the two hemmed edges to create an 11" square; baste the overlapped edges together.

Right sides together, lay the basted square onto the appliquéd square; pin. With the single-welt cording foot installed, stitch the backing square to the appliquéd square. Trim the corners and finish the raw edges with a three-step zigzag.

Turn the pillowcase right side out and insert a pillow form. ✄

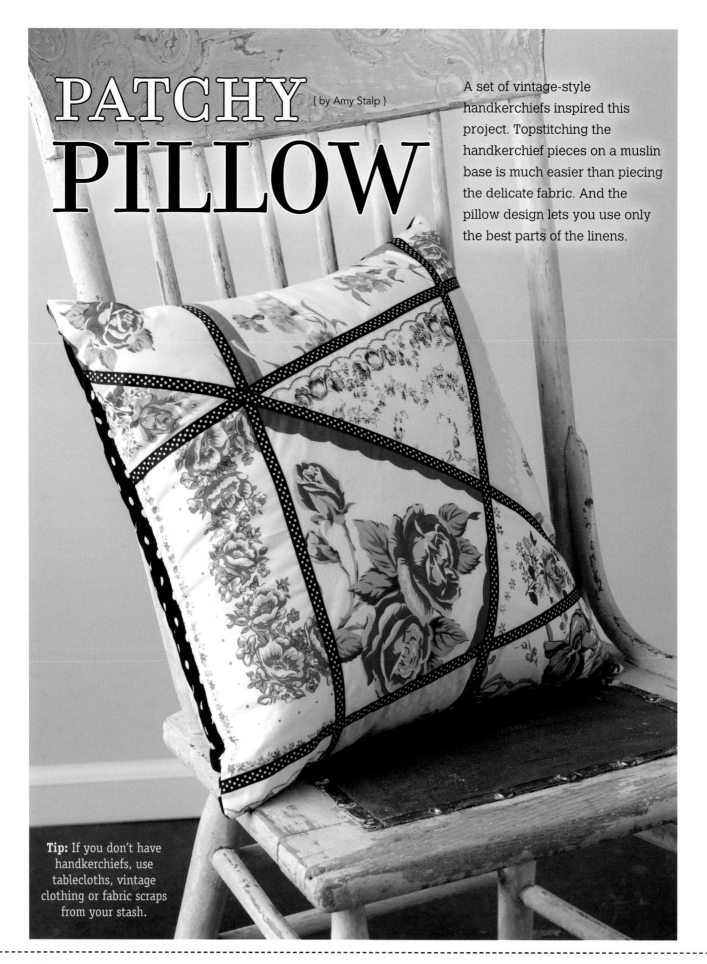

PATCHY
PILLOW

{ by Amy Stalp }

A set of vintage-style handkerchiefs inspired this project. Topstitching the handkerchief pieces on a muslin base is much easier than piecing the delicate fabric. And the pillow design lets you use only the best parts of the linens.

Tip: If you don't have handkerchiefs, use tablecloths, vintage clothing or fabric scraps from your stash.

Tip: If the handkerchiefs are especially delicate, spray them with starch before cutting to stabilize the fabric.

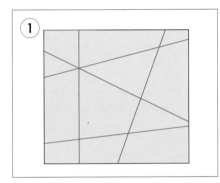

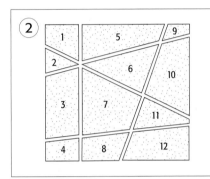

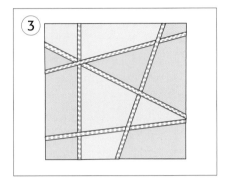

Supplies

- ½ yard of muslin
- Handkerchiefs (approximately 7)
- ³⁄₈"-wide ribbon (amount varies based on design; the featured pillow required 2½ yards)
- ½ yard of backing fabric
- ½ yard of fusible interfacing
- 16"-square pillow form
- Fabric-marking pencil
- All-purpose thread to match muslin and ribbon

Cut & Construct

Cut one 17" square each from the muslin, interfacing and backing fabric. Fuse the interfacing to the muslin wrong side following the manufacturer's instructions. Set aside the backing square.

Position ribbon lengths over the muslin square right side, rearranging until pleased with the design. Using a fabric marker, draw a line to mark each ribbon position **(1)**.

Using a light box or window, trace each drawn section on paper. Number the sections and cut them out **(2)**. Use the paper patterns to cut handkerchief pieces to fit each section.

Right side up, position each handkerchief piece on the muslin, abutting the fabric pieces. Baste the fabric sections in place.

Position the ribbon along the handkerchief edges, making sure the ribbon covers the fabric raw edges and the drawn lines. Edgestitch each ribbon lengthwise edge **(3)**. Remove any visible basting stitches.

Right sides facing, stitch the pillow front and back together, leaving an opening for turning.

Turn the pillow right side out. Insert the pillow form, and hand stitch the opening closed. ✀

CREATIVE OPTIONS

There are lots of different ways to personalize this project to really make it reflect your personal style. Try one of these options or come up with some of your own:

- Attach vintage or funky buttons at the ribbon intersections.
- Use fabric from garments you love but no longer wear. Or use fabric salvaged from thrift- and/ or vintage-store finds.
- Use lace or other trim instead of ribbon.
- Layer different width ribbons.
- Add beads, crystals or sequins.
- Do free-motion quilting over the entire pillow front using matching or contrasting thread.
- Use a colored base fabric that will show through the handkerchiefs.

SILK
sachets

{ by Amy Stalp }

These little silk sachets are great for freshening up drawers.
Tie several together with a pretty bow for a quick and easy gift.

Supplies

Supplies listed are enough to make one sachet.

- Silk fabric (amounts depend on design)
- Pencil and paper
- Matching all-purpose thread
- Hand sewing needle
- Dried lavender or potpourri

Cut & Construct

On the paper, draw a 3″x5″ rectangle. Draw lines across the rectangle to form a design. Use the photo at left for inspiration or come up with your own design. Label each section A, B, C, etc (1). Cut out the sections.

Tape each section to another piece of paper or trace around each section. Using a ruler, add a ¼″ seam allowance to each side of each pattern piece (2). Cut out the patterns.

Using a different color silk for each section, cut out the patterns. Right sides facing and using a ¼″ seam allowance, stitch the sections together to form the sachet front. Press open the seams. Cut a 3½″x5½″ rectangle for the sachet back.

Right sides facing, pin the sachet front and back together. Using a ¼″ seam, stitch around the sachet perimeter, leaving an opening for turning (3).

Clip the corners, and turn the sachet right side out. Press the sachet, turning in the opening edges.

Fill the sachet with dried lavender or potpourri. Slipstitch the opening closed. ✂

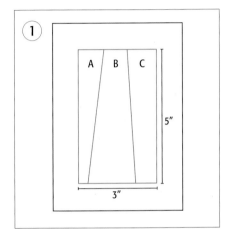

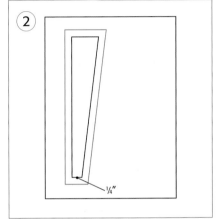

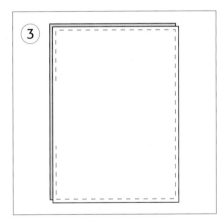

GET IN LINE

If you're using a very delicate or transparent fabric for the sachet, make a lining from muslin to prevent see-through and protect the fabric.

- Cut two 3½″x5½″ rectangles from muslin.
- Right sides facing, pin the rectangles together.
- Using a ¼″ seam, stitch around the rectangle perimeter, leaving an opening for turning.
- Clip the corners, and turn the lining right side out. Press, turning in the opening edges.
- Insert the lining into the sachet before filling it. Hand stitch the lining opening closed, and then stitch the sachet closed.

PERSONALIZE IT

Hand or machine embroider a design on the sachet front before stitching it to the back.

- Stitch beads, sequins or buttons to the sachet.
- Add big hand stitching along the seams on the sachet front.
- Piece both the front and back of the sachet.

Combine style and comfort by making trendy tufted floor pillows. The 8″ thickness and 25″ diameter make them the perfect size for any room.

FLOOR
SEATING

{ by Carol Zentgraf }

Supplies

Supplies listed are enough to make one 25"-diameter, 8"-thick pillow.

- 1¼ yards of 60"-wide decorator fabric or 1 yard of main fabric & ¼ yard of contrasting fabric
- Polyester fiberfill
- 4¾ yards each of ³/₁₆"- wide fusible piping & single-fold bias binding
- Two 1⅛"-diameter covered buttons
- Thread: all purpose & waxed button
- 12"-long upholstery needle

Cut & Prepare

From the fabric, cut two 26"-diameter circles.

For a single matching-fabric side panel, cut one 9"x60" strip and one 9"x24" strip from the fabric.

If using contrasting fabric for the side panel, cut enough 9"-wide strips in assorted lengths from the contrasting fabric to total 83" long when pieced, allowing for ½" seam allowances.

Press open the bias tape.

Construct

Use ½" seam allowances.

Wrap the binding wrong side around the piping; press to fuse, following the manufacturer's instructions, leaving 5" unfused at each end. Trim the seam allowance to ½". Cut the piping length in half.

Position one piping length along one circle right-side perimeter, aligning the raw edges. Using a zipper foot and beginning 1" from the piping end, stitch ½" from the edge (1). To join the piping ends, end the stitching approximately 5" from the piping beginning. Unfold the binding covering and trim the cording even with the piping beginning. Fold the free binding end ¼" toward the wrong side, and then insert it under the piping beginning. Refold the binding around the cording and continue stitching. Repeat to stitch piping to the remaining circle.

With right sides together, piece the side-panel strips along the 9" edges, if applicable.

With right sides together, align one side-panel long edge with one circle edge; pin. Beginning 2" from one side-panel end, stitch along the piping stitching line. When you reach the

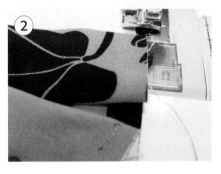

beginning, turn the side-strip end ½" toward the wrong side, insert under the beginning end, and then continue stitching (2). Continue stitching the side panel in place. Repeat to stitch the remaining side-panel long edge to the remaining circle edge.

Turn the pillow right side out through the side panel opening; press. Firmly stuff the pillow with polyester fiberfill. Slipstitch the opening closed.

Finish

Pin-mark each circle center.

Cover the buttons with fabric, follow-ing the manufacturer's instructions.

Cut a 20" length of waxed button thread. Slide one button shank to the thread center. Insert the thread ends through the upholstery needle eye.

Insert the needle into the pillow at one pin mark (3). Bring the needle end out at the opposite pin mark.

Remove the needle and insert one thread end through the remaining

button shank (4). Tie the thread ends together and pull to tuft the pillow center as desired. Securely knot the thread ends several times. Trim the excess thread even with the button underside. ✄

SOURCES

Clover Needlecraft provided the Wrap 'n Fuse Piping: (800) 233-1703, clover-usa.com.

Fairfield Processing Corp. provided the Poly-Fil polyester fiberfill: (800) 980-8000, poly-fil.com.

Prym Consumer USA provided the Cover Button Kits, upholstery needle and waxed button thread: dritz.com.

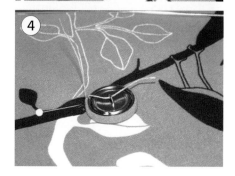

PIPING PARTICULARS

Make custom piping or welting by covering cotton filler cord with bias-cut fabric strips. Cotton cording is available in sizes ranging from $5/32''$ to $1\,3/4''$, so choose a size that's proportionate for your project.

To determine how many yards of strips a fabric square will yield, multiply the square size by itself, divide this number by the strip width, and then divide again by 36". For example, to determine how many 3"-wide strips a 30" fabric square will yield: 30"x 30" =900"; 900"/3"=300"; 300"/36"=8.33 or 8⅓ yards.

To determine the piping length needed, measure the edge where it will be applied, and then add several inches for an overlap.

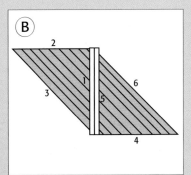

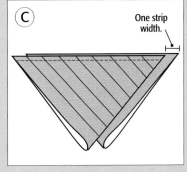

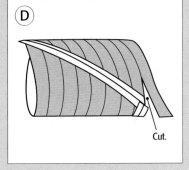

To determine the bias-strip width needed to cover the cording, wrap a tape measure around the cording, and then add 1" to the measurement for seam allowances. Stitch the bias strip ends with right sides together to form one continuous strip.

To make continuous bias strips without having to stitch each end individually, cut them from a fabric square. Determine the fabric square size, and then cut the square in half diagonally. Use a removable fabric marker to number the triangle sides **(A).**

With right sides together, stitch edges 1 and 5 using a ¼" seam allowance. Press open the seam. Beginning at one diagonal edge, use a clear ruler and fabric marker to draw lines indicating the strip width **(B).** Trim the excess fabric beyond the last full-width strip you're able to mark.

Align edges 2 and 4 with right sides together, offsetting them by one strip width; stitch, using a ¼" seam allowance **(C).** Press open the seam.

Beginning at the offset end, cut along the marked lines **(D).**

Wrap the binding around the cording with wrong sides together. Using a welting or zipper foot, baste ⅛" from the cording edge.

SNUGGLE BUG

{ by Halina Salwach }

Make a fuzzy caterpillar neck pillow that'll tickle a youngster's imagination.

Supplies

- 16"x30" fleece rectangle
- 12" square of mediumweight knit
- Green, blue and white felt scraps
- 4 yards of ⁵⁄₈"-wide grosgrain ribbon
- 6 to 8 ounces of polyester fiberfill
- Fabric-marking pen or tailor's chalk
- Fabric glue

Getting Started

Enlarge the caterpillar body pattern on pages 46–47 as directed. Trace and cut out all patterns on pages 45–47.

Right sides together, fold the fleece rectangle in half lengthwise and position the caterpillar body pattern on the foldline; pin and cut out the body.

Transfer the ribbon placement lines and markings to the fleece right side; transfer the tuck and leg slit placement lines to the fleece wrong side. Cut open the leg slits.

Construct

Use ¹⁄₄" seam allowances unless otherwise noted.

Cut a piece of ribbon the length of the first ribbon placement line on the fleece body. Center the ribbon on the placement line and edgestitch. Repeat to stitch the ribbon to the remaining placement lines.

To create the underside tucks, meet each set of tuck lines around each ribbon on the fleece right side. Stitch the tucks together on the wrong side for the length of the tuck line (1).

Cut out the front and back head pieces from the remaining knit. Transfer all markings to the fabric wrong side. Set aside.

Fold the remaining knit in half with right sides together. Pin and cut four leg pairs.

Stitch each leg pair right sides together using a scant ¹⁄₄" seam allowance. Trim the seam allowance to ¹⁄₈", and then turn the legs right side out. Insert a leg into each leg slit, arranging the legs so they curve toward the body. The legs should extend 1¹⁄₄" on the caterpillar right side.

Beginning at the neckline raw edge, stitch across the fleece next to the leg openings. Backstitch across the leg openings for added security (2).

Right sides together, use a ¹⁄₂" seam allowance to stitch the caterpillar body's outside curve. Taper the seam allowance to the large dots, and then backstitch at each dot. Leave the seam open where indicated for turning and stuffing.

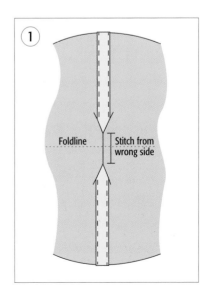

Foldline   Stitch from wrong side

From the green felt, cut out three leaves and arrange them in a diagonal cluster. (For a ridged effect, cut out the leaves with pinking shears.) Align the leaf cluster with the small dot on the front head piece right side. The leaf tips should point toward the head center. Baste the leaf cluster ¼″ from the edge, trim any excess felt even with the head piece raw edge (3).

Right sides facing, stitch the two short ends of the back-head piece. With right sides together, align the small and large dots on the head front and back pieces. Stitch the pieces together, and then turn the head right side out.

Right sides together, position the head inside the fleece body. Match the small dot on the body to the small dot on the head and the large dot on the body to the large dot on the head. Stitch the head to the body, and then turn the caterpillar right side out.

Stuff the caterpillar with fiberfill, and then hand stitch the opening closed.

Cut out the eyes from the white and blue felt pieces. Glue the smaller blue ovals to the larger white ovals. Overlap the eyes, and then stitch or glue them onto the head. ✄

FOR EVEN MORE SNUGGLE FUN, TRY THESE IDEAS:

- Cut two 3½″x5½″ rectangles from muslin.

- Use floral decorator fabric instead of fleece.

- Substitute a silk flower for the leaves.

- Use buttons for the eyes.

- Add extra legs and soon you've got a centipede!

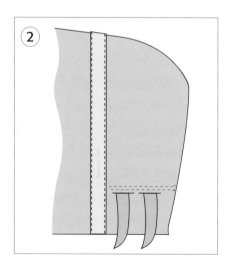

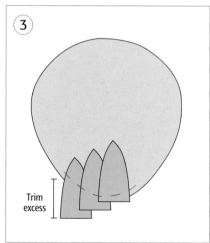

Trim excess

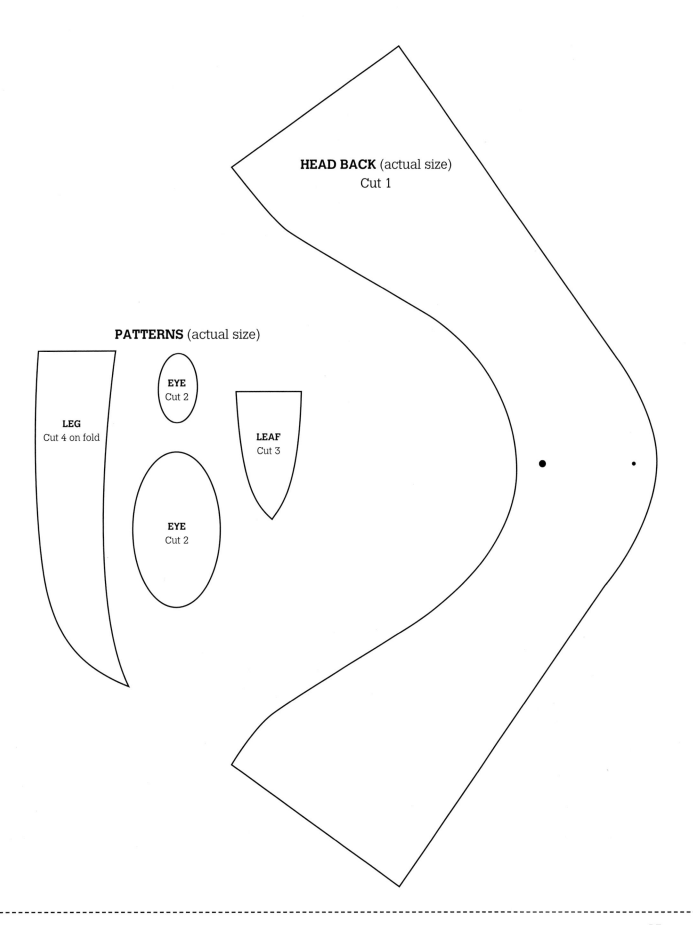

HEAD BACK (actual size)
Cut 1

PATTERNS (actual size)

LEG
Cut 4 on fold

EYE
Cut 2

LEAF
Cut 3

EYE
Cut 2

HEAD FRONT (actual size)
Cut 1

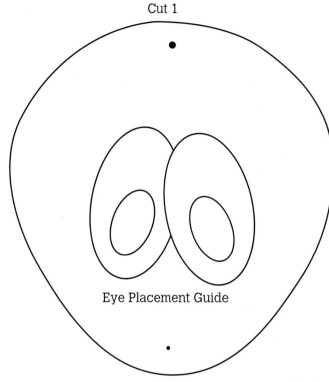

Eye Placement Guide

BODY PATTERN
Reduced 50% of actual size—enlarge 200%

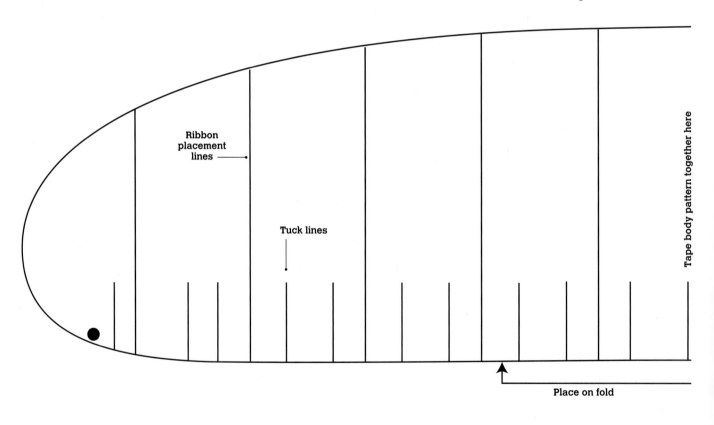

Ribbon
placement
lines

Tuck lines

Tape body pattern together here

Place on fold

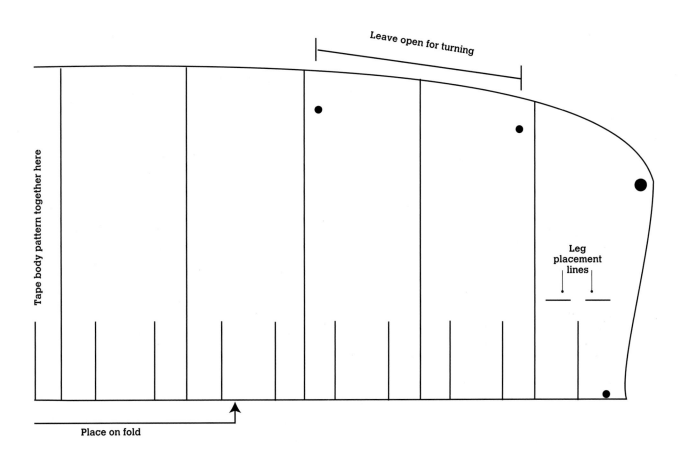

Leave open for turning

Tape body pattern together here

Place on fold

Leg placement lines

stars & stripes

{ by Lois Dahlin }

Give your décor a patriotic kick with a quick-to-make bolster pillow. The pillow cover is removable, so you can easily change it for a festive update.

Supplies

- ²/₃ yard of red-and-white striped cotton fabric
- ¼ yard of blue cotton fabric
- 18"-long bolster pillow form
- All-purpose thread (white, blue)
- Wire garland with red, white and silver stars
- Air-soluble fabric-marking pen

Cut & Construct

From the striped fabric, cut one $19\frac{1}{2}$"x36" rectangle with the stripes running lengthwise. From the blue fabric, cut three 2"x$19\frac{1}{2}$" strips.

Fold one blue strip in half lengthwise with right sides facing; press. Open the strip and fold the long edges to meet

at the center crease; press **(1)**. Repeat for the remaining strips.

Fold the striped rectangle in half crosswise, aligning the 19½″ edges; press. Unfold the fabric.

Position one blue strip with the raw edges facing the striped fabric right side and centered over the fabric center crease; pin.

Draw a line on the striped fabric 3½″ from and parallel to each center strip edge. Center the remaining strips over the lines; pin.

Using blue thread, topstitch along each strip long edge **(2)**.

Set the machine for a 4.0 mm-wide decorative stitch. Using white thread, stitch down each strip center.

Serge-finish the rectangle long edges. Fold the 19½″ edges 4″ toward the wrong side; press. Zigzag stitch close to the raw edges to create a 4″-wide hem **(3)**.

Fold the rectangle in half lengthwise with right sides facing. Stitch the raw edges using a ½″ seam allowance to form a tube.

Turn the tube right side out. Insert the pillow form so that it's centered in the tube.

Hand gather 4″ of the pillow cover fabric at one pillow end. Wrap a 20″ length of garland tightly around the gathers; twist together to secure. Wrap the garland ends around your finger to curl them. Repeat for the other pillow end. ✂

Tip: Make a new bolster pillow cover to decorate for each holiday or season. For a Christmas pillow cover, use red or green velvet and embellish with gold ribbon. For a springtime cover, use seersucker and bright grosgrain ribbon.

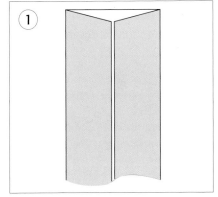

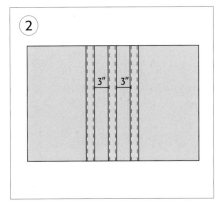

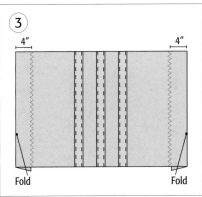

OUTDOOR Décor

{ by Lynne Farris }

Making a custom fabric-covered foam cushion is a great way to update the look of an outdoor bench. Here are some ideas for cutting and shaping the foam and designing the cover to create the perfect cushion to match the bench style.

Cut it Out

Oftentimes, the store employee can cut the foam to size if you know the bench dimensions when you buy. If you'd like to cut it yourself, mark the foam using a soft pencil and a straight edge, and then carefully cut along the lines using a serrated knife. Or use an electric carving knife for easier, quicker cutting. Whether using a serrated or electric knife, cut with the blade perpendicular to the foam to ensure a straight edge and professional result (1).

Box-Style Cushion

Make a tailored box-style bench cushion.

Measure the length and width of the bench seating area; record, and then add 1″ to each measurement.

From the fabric, cut two rectangles according to the bench seat measurements and one gusset strip 1″ wider than the cushion measurements and long enough to fit around the cushion; add a ¼″ seam allowance to the strip diameter. (Piece fabric strips together as necessary to create one 1″-wide strip.)

To create ties, cut two 2″x18″ strips from the fabric. With right sides together, fold one strip in half lengthwise; press. Stitch the long edge using a ¼″ seam. Turn the tube inside out. Fold the raw ends ¼″ toward the wrong side; hand stitch the openings closed. Repeat to stitch the remaining tie.

Pin one tie center at one cover corner, between the lower and side edges; stitch. Pin the remaining tie at the opposite corner; stitch (2).

With right sides together, pin the strip along one rectangle perimeter, and then stitch using a ¼″ seam allowance. Clip the strip at each corner to pivot the stitching line.

Repeat to stitch the remaining rectangle to the opposite strip long edge. Leave an 8″ opening for turning. Trim the corners and press open the seam allowances (3).

Turn the cover right side out. Fold the foam cushion in half to fit inside the opening, and then insert the cushion into the cover. Unfold the foam and align the foam corners with the cover corners.

Slipstitch the opening closed.

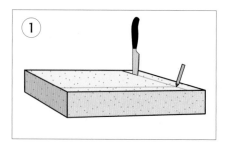

①

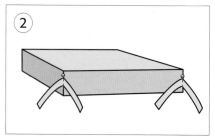

②

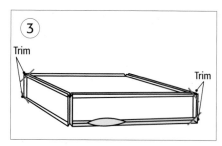

③ Trim   Trim

Tip: Take precise measurements multiple times to ensure the cushion fits the chair or bench perfectly.

Knife-Edge Cushion

For a softer finished look with less loft, create a knife-edge cushion for the bench.

Measure the length and width of the bench seating area; record, and then add 2″ to the perimeter. Cut the foam according to the measurements.

Working in a well-ventilated area, spray foam adhesive on the foam corners, following the manufacturer's instructions. When the glue is dry, pinch the upper and lower foam edges together (4).

Measure the cushion; record, and then add ½″ to each measurement.

From the fabric, cut two rectangles according to the cushion measurements and one strip 1″ wider than the cushion measurements, and long enough to fit around the cushion. Add ½″ seam allowances to the perimeter. (Piece fabric strips together as necessary to create one strip.)

To create ties, cut two 2″x18″ strips from the fabric. With right sides together, fold one strip in half lengthwise; press. Stitch the long edge using a ¼″ seam. Turn the tube right side out. Fold the raw ends ¼″ to the wrong side; hand stitch the openings closed. Repeat to stitch the remaining tie.

Pin one tie center at one cover corner, between the lower and side edges; stitch. Pin the remaining tie at the opposite corner; stitch.

Stitch the strip to the rectangles as per the Box-Style cushion instructions.

To decrease bulk, gradually increase the seam allowance to 1″ at each corner (5).

Trim the corners and press open the seam allowances. Turn the cover right side out.

Fold the foam cushion in half to fit within the opening, and then insert it into the cover. Unfold the foam and align the foam corners with the cover corners.

Slipstitch the opening closed. ✄

THE RIGHT STUFF

Purchase suitable high-density cushion foam from an upholstery supply store or fabric store.

Select the appropriate fabric for the cushion. If the bench is outdoors, use an outdoor fabric that can withstand the elements, such as Sunbrella. If the bench is indoors, select a durable fabric, such as denim, corduroy or heavyweight cotton.

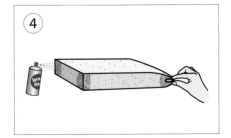

④

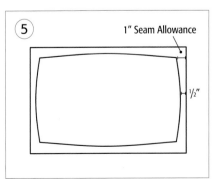

⑤ 1″ Seam Allowance

½″

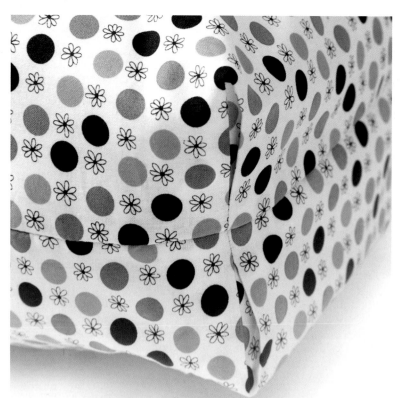

cool corners

{ by Trenia Bell }

Eliminate sharp pillow corners by incorporating Turkish corners into your projects.

A Turkish corner (also known as a butterfly or mock box corner) flattens out a corner seam. It eliminates the right angles that produce those sharp points. As an added bonus, trims don't need to make a sharp curve or bend when stitched to the seamline and your pillow will look thicker.

Cut & Construct

Pinch a corner of the pillow form at the point where it starts to get full (1). Measure the distance from the pinch point to the tip of the corner. Add ½″ to the measurement for a seam allowance.

Cut the pillow front and back pieces. Measuring from each corner, make a mark at the distance determined above (2).

Right sides facing, fold one of the pillow pieces on the diagonal; align the marks. Stitch a straight line perpendicular to the fabric edge beginning at the mark and continuing 1″ into the pillow fabric (3). Repeat to create the remaining corners on both the front and back pillow pieces.

Flatten each corner and center the excess fabric with the seamline; staystitch (4). Trim the excess fabric even with the fabric edge.

Stitch decorative trim along the pillow-front edges if desired. Align the front and back corner seams; stitch, leaving an opening for turning. Turn the fabric right side out. Insert the pillow form, making sure the corners are even. Hand stitch the opening closed. ✄

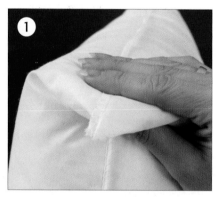

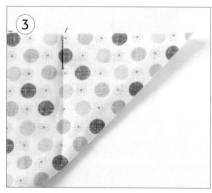

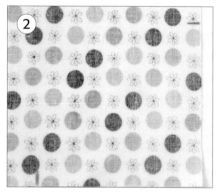

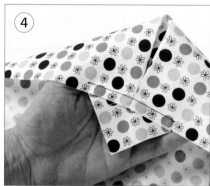

Borders & Banding

{ by Pam Damour }

Add mitered banding or a border to throw pillows for an easy contemporary makeover.

Mitered Banding
Supplies

- 18½" square of home-décor fabric
- 18½" square of coordinating home-décor fabric (plus ¼ yard)
- 16"-long regular zipper
- 17" square pillow form
- Removable fabric marker
- Edge joining or stitch-in-the-ditch foot
- Home-décor ruler or ruler with 45° angle line at the corner (See "Sources.")
- Rotary cutting system (optional)

Prepare

From the coordinating home-décor fabric, cut enough 4"-wide bias strips to create 68" of continuous binding. Piece together the strips using a ¼" seam allowance.

Fold the binding strip in half lengthwise with wrong sides together; press, and then unfold. Fold each long edge toward the center foldline; press.

Construct

With right sides together, fold the home-décor fabric square in half lengthwise and widthwise; finger-press. Mark ½" seam allowances on the square right side, using a removable fabric marker or pencil. Mark the center on each square edge line. Connect the center marks to create a diamond shape (1). Designate one diamond corner as the upper corner.

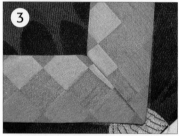

Install an edge joining or stitch-in-the-ditch foot onto the machine and position the needle to the left of the presser foot rudder.

Position the binding long edge along the upper-right line, extending the binding short end 2" beyond the upper corner; pin. Topstitch along the binding outer edge, beginning 2" from the upper corner and ending 2" before the adjacent corner.

Unfold the binding along the outer edge. Fold the binding strip back over itself with right sides together, aligning the short folded edge with the adjacent line; pin. Align the ruler long edge with the seam allowance line and the 45° angle line with the binding outer-edge foldline; mark the binding **(2)**.

Stitch along the marked line. Trim the seam allowance to ½", and then turn the binding toward the right side; press. Fold the binding outer edge toward the wrong side, aligning the outer edges with the lines **(3)**. Continue topstitching the binding outer edge, mitering the next two corners.

End the stitching 2" before the binding beginning. Trim the binding end 2" beyond the upper corner. Align the binding beginning and end with right sides together; pin. Align the ruler long edge with the seam allowance line and the ruler 45° angle line with the binding outer-edge foldline; mark the binding.

Stitch along the marked line. Trim to a ½" seam allowance, and then turn the binding toward the right side; press.

Fold the binding outer edge toward the wrong side. Continue topstitching the binding outer edge.

Position the needle to the right of the presser foot rudder. Topstitch the binding inner edge **(4)**.

With right sides together, stitch the fabric and coordinating fabric perimeter, leaving one edge open for the zipper. Insert the zipper into the opening, following the manufacturer's instructions. Turn the pillow right side out through the zipper opening; press. Insert a pillow form.

Mitered Border
Supplies

- 18½" square of home-décor fabric
- 18½" square of coordinating home-décor fabric (plus ¼ yard)
- 16"-long regular zipper
- 17" square pillow form
- Removable fabric marker
- Edge joining or stitch-in-the-ditch foot
- Home-décor ruler or ruler with 45° angle line at the corner (See "Sources.")
- Rotary cutting system (optional)

Prepare

From the coordinating home-décor fabric, cut enough 4"-wide bias strips to create 86" of continuous binding. Piece together the strips using a ¼" seam allowance.

Fold the binding in half lengthwise with wrong sides together; press.

Construct

Position the home-décor fabric square wrong side up on a flat work surface. Mark ½" seam allowances at each corner, using a removable fabric marker or pencil.

Install an edge joining foot or stitch-in-the-ditch foot onto the machine and position the needle to the right of the presser foot rudder.

Position the fabric square right side up on a flat work surface. Position the binding strip end at one fabric square corner, aligning the raw edges; pin. Topstitch the binding inner edge, beginning 3" from the corner and ending 3" before the adjacent corner.

From the fabric square wrong side, insert a pin at the seam allowance corner mark. From the fabric square right side, insert another pin at the pin-mark (5). Unfold the binding at the pin-marks, keeping one pin on each binding half.

Align the ruler edges with the pin-marks and the 45° angle line with the binding foldline; mark the binding (6). With right sides together, fold the binding in half widthwise ¼" from the binding markings.

Stitch along the marked line. Trim the seam allowance to ½" and clip into the corner (7). Turn the binding to the right side; press. Fold the binding along the foldline with wrong sides together, aligning the outer edge with the square edge (8). Continue topstitching the binding inner edge, mitering the next two corners.

End the stitching 3" before the binding beginning. Trim the binding at the fabric square corner.

From the fabric square wrong side, insert a pin at the seam allowance corner mark. From the fabric square right side, insert another pin at the pin-mark. Unfold the binding at the pin-marks, keeping one pin on each binding half.

Align the ruler edges with the pin-marks and the 45° angle line with the binding foldline; mark the binding. With right sides together, fold the binding in half widthwise ¼" from the marking end points. Repeat to mark the opposite binding end.

Align the binding beginning and end with right sides together, matching the marks; pin. Stitch along the marked line. Trim the seam allowance to ½" and clip into the corner. Turn the binding toward the right side; press. Fold the binding along the foldline with wrong sides together. Continue topstitching the binding inner edge.

With right sides together, stitch the fabric and coordinating fabric square perimeter, leaving one edge open for the zipper. Insert the zipper into the opening, following the manufacturer's instructions. Turn the pillow right side out through the zipper opening; press. Insert a pillow form. ✄

SOURCE
The Decorating Diva carries a home-décor ruler: (518) 297-2699, pamdamour.com.

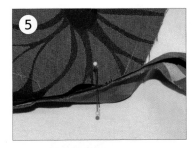

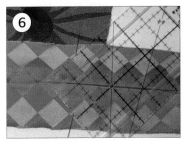

ZIP TO IT

{ by Pam Damour }

There are several ways to install a zipper into a pillow, depending on the pillow style and trims.

Always use a home-décor zipper, not a clothing zipper or invisible zipper, as they aren't sturdy enough for professional home-décor sewing. Home-décor zippers are available in multiple colors to match any project and long lengths with separate slides, so the exact zipper length can be cut without waste.

Lower-Edge Zipper

Inserting a zipper into the project lower edge is the easiest application for a completely concealed zipper. Use this application for a pillow without trim.

From the fabric, cut one pillow front and back according to the desired pillow size plus seam allowance. Designate a lower edge on the pillow front and back.

Cut the desired zipper length, including seam allowances. Close the zipper and remove the zipper pull.

Install a zipper foot onto the machine. With right sides together,

stitch the left zipper tape to the pillow-front lower edge beginning at the zipper-tape upper edge (1). Repeat

to stitch the right zipper tape to the pillow-back lower edge.

Separate the zipper teeth 3″ to 4″ along the upper edge. Insert the zipper pull onto the zipper tape. Align the slider to each zipper-tape teeth end and zip the zipper **(2)**. Slide the pull to the pillow lower-edge center.

With right sides together, stitch the pillow front and back perimeter, backstitch at the zipper upper and lower ends to secure. Trim the pillow corners and serge- or zigzag-finish the seams.

Trim the pillow corners, and then turn right side out through the zipper opening; press.

Placket Zipper

Use a placket application with a flange pillow or to install the zipper along, but not in, the lower-edge seam.

From the fabric, cut one pillow front and back according to the desired pillow size plus seam allowance. Designate a lower edge on the pillow front and back

For a standard placket, cut one rectangle measuring 2″ x the pillow-back width along the same grainline as the pillow-back lower edge. For a flange pillow placket, cut one rectangle measuring the flange width plus 1″ x

the pillow-back width. Designate one placket long edge as the upper edge.

Fold the placket upper edge ½″ toward the wrong side; press. Fold the back pillow lower edge ½″ toward the wrong side; press **(3)**. Serge- or zigzag-finish the pillow perimeter.

Cut the zipper tape to the needed length. Close the zipper and remove the zipper slide. Position the zipper right side up on a flat work surface. Position the placket upper edge right side up over the left zipper tape,

aligning the folded edge with the zipper teeth; pin. Install a zipper foot onto the machine. Topstitch the placket close to the folded edge **(4)**.

With right sides facing up, position the pillow-back lower edge over the right zipper tape, extending the folded edge ¼″ over the zipper teeth; pin. Topstitch the back pillow ⅜″ from the folded edge **(5)**.

Separate the zipper teeth 3″ to 4″ along the upper edge. Insert the zipper pull onto the zipper tape **(6)**. Align the

slider to each zipper-tape teeth end and close the zipper. Slide the pull to the pillow lower-edge center.

Align the pillow front and back with right sides together. Trim the pillow front perimeter evenly with the pillow back perimeter. Stitch the pillow front and back perimeter, backstitching at the zipper upper and lower ends to secure. Trim the pillow corners and serge- or zigzag-finish the seams.

Trim the pillow corners, and then turn right side out through the zipper opening; press.

If creating a flange pillow, topstitch the pillow perimeter according to the flange width.

Zipper Between Two Trims

Use a lower-edge insertion between two trims to create an inconspicuous zipper.

From the fabric, cut one pillow front and back according to the desired pillow size plus seam allowance. Designate a lower edge on the pillow front and back.

From the trim, cut two lengths according to the pillow perimeter plus seam allowance.

Install a zipper foot onto the machine. Stitch one trim length onto the pillow

front perimeter. Repeat to stitch the remaining trim length onto the pillow back perimeter.

Cut the desired zipper length, including seam allowances. Separate the zipper and remove the zipper pull.

Position the pillow front right side up on a flat work surface. Position the left zipper tape wrong side up over the pillow lower edge, aligning the zipper tape and pillow raw edges; pin, and then stitch close to the zipper teeth (7). Repeat to stitch the right zipper tape to the pillow-back lower edge.

Align the slider to each zipper-tape teeth end and close the zipper, removing the slide at the opposite zipper end. Open the zipper teeth along the upper edge 3″ to 4″. Realign the slider with the zipper-teeth ends (8). Slide the pull to the pillow lower-edge center.

Install a 100/16 or 110/18 denim needle onto the machine. With right sides together, stitch the pillow front and back perimeter, backstitch at the zipper upper and lower ends to secure. ✁

SOURCE

The Decorating Diva carries home-dec zippers: (518) 297-2699, pamdamour.com.

DINING
Décor

{ by Lynne Farris }

Update the look and padding of dining room chairs for a simple home makeover.

Prepare

Select foam made from compressed polyester fiber, such as NU-Foam. Compressed polyester fiber is a better material than traditional polyurethane foam because it's flame-retardant, mildew-resistant, washable and non-allergenic, and it won't yellow or disintegrate over time. It's available in several precut sizes and thicknesses that are designed specifically for chairs.

Turn the chair upside down. Unscrew the screws holding the seat in place. Using a heavy-duty staple remover, carefully loosen and remove each cushion staple.

Remove the existing foam pad. It's likely that the foam pad began to disintegrate over time, so use care when removing the foam from the cover. Discard the foam pad.

Create a pattern using the existing seat fabric. Press the fabric, and then position it over a large piece of butcher paper. Using a marker, trace the shape onto the paper; cut out. Discard the fabric.

Construct

Position the new seat fabric right side up on a flat work surface. Using a removable fabric marker, trace the pattern onto the fabric; cut out.

Place the foam on a flat work surface. Position the seat base over the foam. Using a removable fabric marker, trace the seat base onto the foam. Cut along the traced line using sharp scissors or a utility knife. Even when using precut foam, trimming may still be necessary to achieve the correct fit.

Position the fabric right side down on a flat work surface. Center the foam cushion over the fabric, and then place the seat base over the foam (1).

Pull the fabric taut toward the seat base along each side center; staple the fabric to the seat base using a staple gun (2).

Pull the fabric taut toward the seat base along the remaining edges. Work from the center toward the corners, smoothing the fabric as you pull. Fold under the fabric raw edges, and then staple. Finish the corners by making a small pleat, and then staple the fabric edges to the seat base (3).

Repeat to reupholster each chair cushion. Reattach each chair frame. ✄

SOURCE
Fairfield Processing Corporation carries NU-Foam:
(800) 980-8000, poly-fil.com.

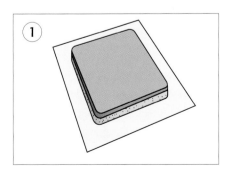

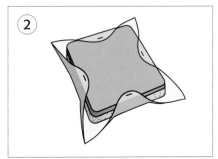

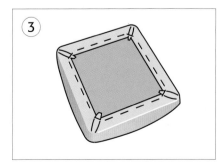

COLORFUL CUSHIONS

{ by Pam Damour }

Creating seat or box cushions is easy once you know a few tricks of the trade.

Supplies

- 3"- thick foam (amount determined by cushion size)
- Upholstery fabric (amount determined by cushion size)
- Bonded Dacron batting (amount determined by cushion size; see "Sources")
- Home-dec zipper by the yard (length determined by cushion size; see "Sources")
- ¼"-diameter welt cording (amount determined by cushion; see "Sources")
- All-purpose thread
- Presser feet: welt cord (optional) & zipper
- Electric serrated knife
- Permanent marker
- Spray foam adhesive

Prepare

Measure the length and width of the seating area; record. Double the width measurement; add the length measurement, and then record for the front-rise strip length. Add 8" to the length measurement; record for the back-rise strip length. Add the length and width measurement together, multiply by four, add 4", and then record for the welt cording length.

From the fabric, cut two rectangles according to the recorded length and width measurements; add ½" seam allowance to each rectangle perimeter for the cushion top and bottom panel.

From the fabric, cut one strip measuring 4"x the recorded front-rise strip length and one strip measuring 5"x the recorded back-rise strip length.

From the fabric, cut enough 2"-wide bias strips to equal the welt cord length, including ¼" seam allowances.

Measure and mark the recorded length and width measurements on the foam using a permanent marker. Cut along the lines using an electric serrated knife.

From the batting, cut two rectangles measuring to the recorded length plus 3"x the width plus 3". Cut a 1½" square from each rectangle corner.

Working in a well-ventilated area, spray foam adhesive on the foam cushion following the manufacturer's instructions. Adhere each batting rectangle to the foam cushion (1).

Construct

Fold the bias strip in half lengthwise with wrong sides together; unfold. Center one welt cording length over the foldline along the fabric wrong side. Fold the strip in half lengthwise with wrong sides together, concealing the cording. Install a welt cord or zipper foot onto the machine. Stitch close to the cording to create welting. Cut the welting in half widthwise.

Position one welting length along the upper-panel right-side perimeter,

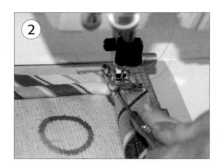

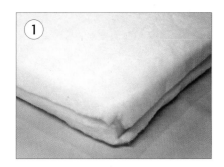

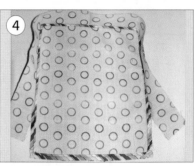

aligning the raw edges. Using a welt cord or zipper foot, stitch $\frac{1}{2}''$ from the edge, beginning 1″ from the welting end. Continue stitching the welting along the panel perimeter, clipping the welting seam allowance up to, but not through, the stitching line at the first corner. Ease the welting around the corner and continue stitching (2).

End the stitching 1″ from the opposite welting end, and then trim the beginning welting end at a 45° angle. Remove the stitches along the welting end, and then trim the cording so the end aligns with the beginning. Turn the welting end $\frac{1}{2}''$ toward the wrong side. Position the fold over the welting beginning; stitch (3). Repeat to stitch the remaining welting to the lower-panel perimeter.

Fold the upper and lower panels and front-rise strip in half widthwise to find the center; press, and then unfold. Designate a center-front and center-back foldline on each panel.

With right sides together, pin the front-rise strip along the upper-panel perimeter, aligning the panel center-front and strip foldlines. Clip the front-rise seam allowance up to, but not through, the seamline at each corner, easing the front-rise strip around each corner.

Begin stitching 6″ from one strip short end, positioning the needle just inside the welting stitching. Continue stitching the strip along the panel perimeter, ending 6″ from the opposite strip short end (4).

Cut the back-rise strip in half lengthwise. Designate one strip as the upper strip and one strip as the lower strip. Designate each strip upper and

lower edge. Fold the upper-strip lower edge and the lower-strip upper edge $\frac{1}{2}''$ toward the wrong side; press.

With right sides facing up, position the lower-strip upper edge over one zipper tape, aligning the strip folded edge with the zipper teeth; stitch using a zipper foot. With right sides facing up, lap the upper-strip lower edge over the opposite zipper tape, abutting the upper- and lower-strip folded edges; stitch using a zipper foot (5).

Fold the back-rise strip in half widthwise to find the center; press, and then unfold. With right sides together, pin the upper strip along the upper-panel perimeter, aligning the panel center-back and strip foldlines. Clip the upper-strip seam allowance up to, but not through, the seamline at each corner, easing the upper strip around each corner; stitch, leaving 2″ unstitched at each short end.

Overlap the front-rise short end over the back-rise short end. Measure and mark $3\frac{1}{2}''$ from the back-rise short end along the front-rise strip; trim along the mark. With right sides together, stitch the back-rise short end to the front-rise short end (6).

With wrong sides together, fold the front rise to create a $1\frac{1}{2}''$ flap on each zipper end; pin. With right sides together, stitch the panel perimeter along the open areas. The flap creates a pocket to protect the zipper slide and prevents the zipper end from ripping out.

With right sides together, pin the lower-panel perimeter to the front- and back-rise perimeter, aligning the foldlines and corners; stitch. Clip the corners (7).

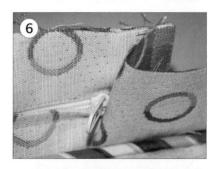

Turn the cover right side out through the zipper opening. Insert the foam cushion into the cover. ✄

SOURCES
DIY Upholstery Supply carries Bonded Dacron batting: (662) 280-0020, diyupholsterysupply.com.
The Decorating Diva carries home-dec zipper by the yard and welt cord: (518) 297-2699, pamdamour.com.

trim TIME

{ by Pam Damour }

There are many different trim varieties available. Learn about the main types and how to use them in pillow projects.

Brush Fringe

Brush fringe is bound on one long edge and the remaining long edge is loose fringe. Brush fringe comes with the fringe loosely chainstitched. Do *not* remove the chainstitching until after attaching the trim to the project. Brush fringe is usually sewn into seams. To connect the ends, abut them, and then stitch over the juncture along the bound edge (1).

Bullion Trim

Bullion trim is available in various lengths and thicknesses. It's a heavier fringed trim and works best on larger projects. Bullion trims are manufactured with different lips, the flat upper edges that holds the trim together. Bullion trim with

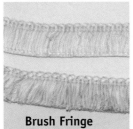

Brush Fringe

Bullion Trim

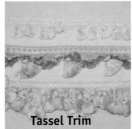

Tassel Trim

Twisted Cord

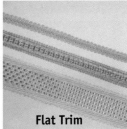

Flat Trim

a decorative lip is either stitched to the project surface or applied using permanent double-sided tape. Fold the cut ends toward the wrong side, and then stitch close to the fold to secure. Bullion trim that has a flat lip is designed to be sewn into a seam. To connect the ends, abut them within the seam, and then stitch along the lip edge.

Tassel Trim

Tassel trims come in wonderful patterns and colors and vary greatly in price. As with bullion trim, tassel trim is stitched into seams or onto the project surface or attached using permanent double-sided tape.

Twisted Cord

Twisted cord is available with or without a lip. The lip is necessary to machine stitch the cord into a project. Cord without a lip can only be hand stitched onto a project.

To stitch twisted cord into a seam, begin with the needle in the center position. Move the needle position until it aligns with the cord and lip juncture. Set the machine to a 3mm-long straight stitch. Begin stitching 2″ from the cord beginning. End stitching 1″ from the stitching beginning. Cut the cord 2″ from the stitching end. Wrap the cut ends with tape to prevent raveling (2).

To connect the twisted cord ends, remove the lip from the cord 1½″ from

each end. Do not cut the lip. Fold the lip ends toward the wrong side (3). Overlap the cord in the direction of the twist (4).

Stitch over the cord juncture in the direction of the twist. Turn the fabric around if necessary (5).

Flat Trim

There are many varieties of flat trim available that add great visual interest to a project. When sewing flat trims, use polyester invisible thread. Always test-stitch the trim to a fabric scrap before stitching the project to determine the appropriate tension settings. If necessary, loosen the upper thread tension when stitching with polyester invisible thread. Do *not* use nylon thread, as it's coarser and will melt when ironed. Or use permanent double-sided tape to apply flat trim to a project surface.

Welt Cord

Purchase welt cord to insert into seams or make your own. To make your own, cut a bias strip according to the desired trim length and wide enough to wrap around the cord, and providing ample seam allowance. Piece strips together to achieve the desired length, if necessary.

Install a welt cord foot onto the machine. Fold the bias strip around the welt cord with wrong sides together, and then place the cord under the

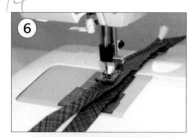

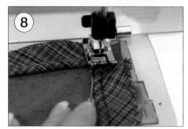

presser foot groove (6). Set the machine to a 3mm-long straight stitch and move the needle two positions to the right. Move the needle as needed depending on the cord width. Don't stitch too close to the cord, as the stitching line may show after the cord is stitched into the project. Or instead of a welt cord foot, use a zipper foot and move the needle to the furthest left position, aligning the needle with the foot edge.

Once the fabric is stitched around the cord, align the welting raw edge with the fabric raw edge. Stitch the welting to the fabric between the previous stitching line and the cord.

To stitch the welting around a corner, cut the lip to, but not through, the

stitching line $^3/_4$" and $^1/_2$" from the raw edge and at the fabric edge (7). Turn the welting around the corner, aligning the lip raw edge with the adjacent raw edge (8).

With right sides together, align the welted fabric with the corresponding fabric piece; pin. Position the needle in the center and set the machine to a 3mm-long straight stitch. With the welted fabric wrong side up, stitch between the previous stitching lines and the cord. ✂

SOURCE

The Decorating Diva carries welt cord, permanent double-stick tape, DVD 109 "Secrets of a Decorator Workroom" and *Cheaper by the Dozen* by Pam Damour: (518) 297-2699, pamdamour.com.

Template for Autumn Appliqué pillow on page 8.

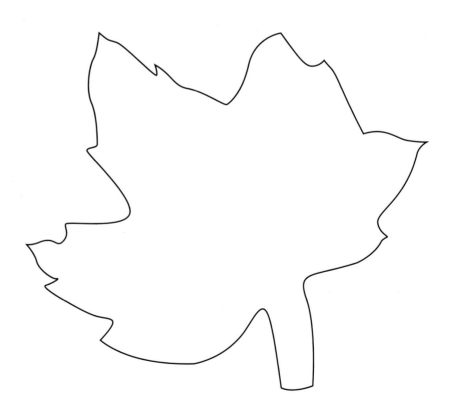